Richard Willey

Race, Equality and Schools

Methuen · London and New York

First published in 1984 by
Methuen & Co. Ltd
11 New Fetter Lane,
London EC4P 4EE

Published in the USA by
Methuen & Co.
in association with Methuen, Inc.
733 Third Avenue, New York,
NY 10017

Typeset in Great Britain by
Activity Limited, Salisbury, Wilts,
Printed in Great Britain by
Richard Clay (The Chaucer Press) Ltd,
Bungay, Suffolk

*British Library Cataloguing in
Publication Data*

*Willey, Richard
Race, equality and schools.
1 Race relations in
school management
I. Title
370.19'342   LC212.5*

ISBN 0-416-38310-6

For Fred and Eleanor

p.27-34

Contents

Introduction
Equality in a multi-ethnic society

How to respond to ethnic diversity in schools and in society is now recognized to raise complex and wide-ranging questions which have general relevance to all teachers. This constitutes a considerable change. Ten years ago the primary preoccupation was with fitting minority ethnic groups into the existing education system. Now attention has turned to achieving equality in a multi-ethnic society. Once this perspective is adopted, teachers are confronted by questions which have far-reaching implications for many aspects of educational practice. For example, to what extent do prejudiced and discriminatory attitudes and practices pervade educational provision? How can teachers combat racism in schools and in society? How should schools respond to cultural and linguistic diversity? How do black children achieve in the educational system and how can their particular educational needs best be met? What are the implications for teachers who are not working in multi-racial schools?

Over recent years such questions have assumed an increasingly central place in general educational discussion. In part, this is because the framework established by formal educational policies has altered. In a number of national educational systems policies of assimilating minority ethnic group pupils have been replaced by 'multi-cultural', pluralist objectives. This has taken place, for example, in Australia, Canada and the United States as well as in Britain. A policy of assimilation seeks to absorb minority ethnic groups into the existing education system. Broadly, it is the pupil who must adapt and change, not the school, and there are minimal implications for mainstream teaching. A pluralist approach, on the other hand, involves schools responding positively to the fact that society as a whole comprises a range of different ethnic and cultural groups. Teaching about the diverse nature of society and about the realities of black-white relations within it becomes of general relevance to all teachers and all pupils.

But in practice response to these new theoretical objectives has often been confined to emphasizing aspects of cultural difference without confronting the effects of racism (racism is a term meaning stereotyping people by race; just as sexism is stereotyping people by sex). 'Multi-cultural' policies have invariably been couched in the bland and safe language of tolerance, harmony and mutual understanding, not in the contentious realities of prejudice and discrimination. This has led to the development of a new perspective which places the primary emphasis not on diversity but on securing equality. This has the effect of focusing attention firmly on the need to develop specific strategies to combat racism. From this base positive responses to ethnic and cultural diversity can be developed.

This book has two main aims. The first is to examine the main issues in the debate about educational response to ethnic diversity. The focus on equality and racism has important implications which have wide relevance for teachers. The second aim is to indicate some of the ways in which a variety of approaches in schools are testing theoretical assumptions and policies against the realities of classroom practice.

Pluralist objectives

At official policy level the conversion to pluralist objectives – at any rate theoretically – has been striking. In Britain post-war immigration from the West Indies, Asia and East Africa has led to the formulation of a range of significantly different policy responses over a relatively short period. Between 1951 and 1971 Britain's black population grew from some 0.5 million to 1.85 million – 3.4 per cent of the total population. Over this period government response shifted from an initial *laissez-faire* approach based on an implicit assumption that the overall objective was assimilation to categoric assertion of the importance of positive approaches to cultural diversity. Initial government reaction was that the immigrants would simply be absorbed into the majority society. No particular social policy response was necessary; any difficulties would, given time and goodwill, take care of themselves. Differences relating to race and cultural background were deliberately played down for fear of arousing resentment and hostility among the majority population and activating a 'white backlash'. But by 1977 the Department of Education and Science (DES) was declaring 'Our society is a multi-cultural, multi-racial one and the curriculum should reflect a sympathetic understanding of the different cultures and races that now make up our society' (DES, 1977). The curriculum in all schools, the Department asserted, 'must reflect the needs of this new Britain'. Over the same period directly comparable developments took place in Canada, Australia and the United States. In Canada the Prime Minister, Pierre Trudeau, announced in 1971 that an earlier ideology of 'Anglo-conformity' had been transformed into 'multi-culturalism within a bi-lingual framework'. In 1975 the

Australian Schools Commission was urging that all schools, regardless of their particular ethnic composition, 'must recognise and value the diversity of Australian society' (Australian Schools Commission, 1975). In the United States in 1972 an amendment to the Education Act was introduced (Title IX) which was intended to introduce into all schools recognition of 'the educational gains that can result from understanding the contributions of cultural pluralism to a multi-ethnic Nation'.

Policy makers have been much more hesitant about spelling out the detailed implications of pluralism than in pronouncing broad objectives. But certain assumptions underlying such aims are clear. The changed ethnic composition of society is recognized to have implications for the members of that society as a whole. The majority population will be affected by changes which have made them part of a society which actively endorses the ethnic and cultural diversity within it. There are two main consequences for teachers. First, a pluralist objective has relevance to the education of all children, and, second, the onus is no longer – as in an assimilationist model – simply on minority ethnic group pupils to adapt to the education system. The system itself has to change both in response to the altered nature of society and to the particular educational needs of minority ethnic group pupils.

Racism and equality

Theoretically, pluralist objectives have far reaching implications for education – for the curriculum, for a wide range of forms of school organization and practice, for teachers' approaches and attitudes. But comprehensive educational change has not resulted from the new objectives. In all the education systems professing pluralist aims there is a uniform gap between policy and practice. A central reason for this is that there has been almost exclusive emphasis on aspects of culture and cultural difference and neglect of the entrenched and pervasive influence of racism. Schools cannot effectively develop positive responses to cultural diversity without confronting the realities of racial discrimination. Attitudes to different cultures are in practice inextricably interwoven with the pervasive effects of past and present racial prejudice. A central and inescapable characteristic of the societies in which teachers are being asked to develop pluralist approaches is that 'the colour of one's skin is an important and visible indicator of one's life chances' (Allen, 1979).

The nature of racism and its effects has been progressively understood. It has been increasingly accepted that black people are not only subjected to individual discriminatory acts but are also disadvantaged as a group through indirect discrimination which operates more as a result of 'institutional practices and patterns than of deliberate acts by prejudiced individuals' (Bindman and Grosz, 1979). Equality for individuals cannot be achieved unless discriminatory practices are removed which affect black people as a group. Racism has, over the centuries, entered deep into the interstices of society, in a comparable way to the operation of sexism. And, as with sexism, systematic and sustained action is necessary to dismantle racism. It is the failure of 'multi-cultural' policies to address the effects of racism which has led to a radical reappraisal of existing responses. In Britain, a new approach has been advocated – 'a perspective emphasising primarily Equality' (ILEA, 1983b). In this context concern centres not on cultural difference but on equality and justice and combating 'the central and pervasive influence of racism'.

Implications for all schools

A consequence of focusing on equality is that it concentrates attention on the extent to which responding to ethnic diversity has implications for a school as a whole. 'Multi-cultural' developments have often in practice been confined to making particular additions to existing teaching which remain largely peripheral to the mainstream curriculum. But concern with equality makes explicit response to racism a natural and integral part of providing good education. As the head of a London comprehensive which has adopted this sort of approach comments:

Add to
H/C.

> I don't really see how you can run a comprehensive school with a mixed social and cultural intake without being explicit about your stance on race. All children are equally important to us in every sense. If racism manifests itself in the school it undermines the learning of some of our children — it breeds insecurity. (ILEA, 1982a)

In this school staff have adopted a policy based on the view that:

> In the staff handbook the first aim of Quintin Kynaston school is to demonstrate that we regard all students as being of equal value. Racism is diametrically opposed to this aim and must therefore be positively resisted by the school. It is important that everyone associated with Quintin Kynaston see the school's policy on racism as a natural part of the responsibilities of a comprehensive school. (ILEA, 1982a)

Another example is a school which has developed its pluralist policies from the 'general principle' that

Add to
H/C

> We must ensure that all our pupils have an equal chance to make good use of the education the school [North Westminster School] offers to enable them to choose their future pattern of life and to take full advantage of their opportunities in society. This means that the school will on every occasion demonstrate within the community its opposition to racism and foster positive attitudes towards our multi-cultural society. These principles must inform and guide every group in the school. (ILEA, 1982a)

Once attention is turned to the 'general principle' of equality, responding to racism — which negates this principle —

becomes not a peripheral matter buried under competing priorities for teachers' attention, but a central issue at the heart of contemporary education. Combating racism is seen not as an additional element which must be built into 'multi-cultural' approaches, but as the core from which responses to diversity must develop.

The need to develop such policies is being recognized in a growing number of multi-racial schools. But in a multi-ethnic society committed to equality the issues being discussed by these teachers are of relevance to all schools. Racism does not manifest itself simply in direct discriminatory acts between white and black people, it is endemic in the attitudes which pervade society. Racist ideology, and the values and beliefs which surround it, is based on the assumption that black people are inferior to white people. Such notions are deeply embedded in the procedures, practices and structures of institutions. The questions discussed in this book have direct relevance to teachers working in all-white schools. Particularly important, for example, are the ways in which teachers are developing systematic procedures to examine the effects of racism both on educational practice and on their own personal attitudes and assumptions. It is in multi-racial schools that the issues are most obviously apparent and have been most clearly identified, but they have relevance to education as a whole.

Indeed, many of the questions which arise in relation to developing responses to ethnic diversity present in an acute form issues which are already of wide concern to teachers. For example, the experience of black pupils within the education system throws into sharp relief wider discussion of equality in education. Combating racism raises important questions for the continuing debate about the relationship of the school and the curriculum it teaches to the values and attitudes prevalent in the wider society. Child-centred views of education take on an added dimension when the concept of building on what the child brings to school is applied in a pluralist context. Responding to minority ethnic groups introduces a new

dimension into developing provision aimed at meeting the
particular needs of some pupils.

In the Inner London Education Authority (ILEA) experience
has shown that schools where successful developments have
taken place are distinguishable by five major characteristics.
These illustrate both the wide implications for schools and the
extent to which effective responses are integral to the general
development of good educational practice. The five characteristics identified by ILEA are: the teachers have clearly
thought-out policies for dealing with racism; there is sensitive
teaching for all pupils and a realization that good relationships
are not enough; high expectations are maintained and there is
sensitive awareness of potential; the curriculum has been
imaginatively developed, often as a result of joint work by the
inspectorate, advisory teachers, and staff from the Teachers'
Centres; links have been established with the community, and
parents – including those from minority groups – take a full
part in the life of the school (ILEA, 1983b).

➤ Add in H/C

Responding to linguistic diversity

A striking example of the way in which response to ethnic
diversity has sharpened perception of an issue which is of
general relevance to all teachers is the way in which the
presence of bilingual children has stimulated the general
debate about linguistic diversity in schools. It is only relatively
recently that it has been considered educationally relevant to
enquire systematically into the linguistic skills of pupils. More
languages are spoken in London than in New York, but it was
only in 1981 that the Inner London Education Authority
carried out its first comprehensive language survey (ILEA,
1982b). This revealed the complexity of the situation facing
teachers in London classrooms. A total of 44,925 pupils –
13.9 per cent of the total ILEA primary and secondary school
population – were identified as using a language other than, or
in addition to, English at home. Foreign language speaking

pupils constituted 16.1 per cent of primary rolls and 11.5 per cent of secondary rolls. A total of 131 different languages were recorded; the twelve main ones, each having over 1000 speakers and together accounting for 82.6 per cent of pupils speaking a language other than English, were, in order of number of speakers, Bengali, Turkish, Greek, Spanish, Gujerati, Punjabi, Italian, Urdu, Chinese, French, Arabic and Portuguese. And this is not all. The ILEA survey did not collect information about English-based creoles, such as Jamaican creole. A smaller-scale survey carried out in 28 schools found not only 58 named world languages represented, but 42 different overseas dialects of English (Rosen and Burgess, 1980).

A decade earlier, working within an assimilationist policy frame, response to such linguistic diversity was seen as a relatively straightforward matter. The children needed to be taught English to equip them to enter normal classes. This would be accomplished by specialist English as a second language (E2L) teachers, often working in centres physically separated from schools. Once the children entered mainstream classes they would be essentially no different from other pupils and the work of most teachers would remain unaffected. But in a pluralist context the position is altered. Working from the basic principle of wishing to build on the experiences that children bring to school, teachers have begun to reconsider how to respond to their bilingual pupils and are often led into new and unexplored territory. An example is a teacher whose question 'Do you have another language you understand?' brought the response from an 11-year-old girl: 'I speak English at school, Gujerati on my way home to my friends. I read books at Mosque in Urdu, and I learn passages from the Koran in Arabic ... my mother speaks Marathi.' The teacher's first reaction was one of anxiety. 'How can the child cope? ... surely she must confuse the different languages?' Yet the child seemed to cope remarkably well. She had no emotional difficulties and her English showed no sign of interference from her other languages. Slowly the teacher began to conclude that perhaps the child's multi-lingual experience had provided her with an 'insight into language' that was 'quite incomprehensible to the monolingual person'. For this teacher this was a starting point from which he could begin to inform himself about his pupils' languages, and consider ways in which they might be given more recognition in the curriculum (Houlton, 1984).

New attitudes to bilingualism relate closely to the wider re-examination of language and education which has taken place in recent years. The important and influential Bullock Report, *A Language for Life*, expressly made a connection between the particular needs of minority ethnic groups and general educational good practice, asserting the principle that

> No child should be expected to cast off the language and culture of the home as he crosses the school threshold, nor to live and act as though school and home represent two totally separate and different cultures which have to be kept firmly apart. (DES, 1975)

Increased language awareness in multi-racial schools has accentuated educational issues which have a wider relevance. Linguistic diversity has always been a phenomenon in schools. The questions raised by the richer diversity of languages and dialects now present in some schools are not new, but they are in the new context much harder to ignore. What is at stake is people's beliefs about the place of language in schools and classrooms, and people's tolerance – or lack of it – not only of children's home languages but of regional and social variation in language (Stubbs, 1976). Language is only one area in which response to ethnic diversity presents in an acute form a central issue confronting contemporary education.

A comparative perspective

As has already been suggested, in Australia, Canada and the United States changing policy approaches to ethnic diversity, and the debates to which they give rise, have been remarkably similar to developments in Britain. This book is primarily about the discussion of the issues and classroom experiences in Britain. But throughout a comparative perspective is maintained. To a considerable degree experience in Britain is relevant elsewhere, and developments in other countries inform and illustrate the debate in Britain.

This is so despite the fact that the particular ethnic composition of the different countries varies considerably. In Canada the 1971 Census showed 44.6 per cent of the population as being identified by ethnicity as British (i.e. from the British Isles), 28.7 per cent French, 1.3 per cent Asiatic and 1.4 per cent native Indian. In Australia in 1975, 25 per cent of the population were post-war immigrants or the children of post-war immigrants; 8.7 per cent were born in non-English speaking European countries, and some 1 per cent were Aborigines or part Aborigines.

In relation to the United States the point has often been made that in general terms the differences between the situation of ethnic minorities there and in Britain are as marked as the similarities (Rutter and Madge, 1976). The 25 million black Americans (so defined in the Census by self-identification) constitute a remarkably homogeneous group, whose origins and present characteristics differentiate them sharply from their relatively recently arrived counterparts in Britain, where ethnic minorities come from a wide range of backgrounds. But useful comparisons can still be drawn. In particular, the development of 'positive discrimination' and 'affirmative action' programmes in the United States have important implications for approaches in other countries.

About this book

This book argues that responding positively to ethnic diversity requires a wide-ranging reappraisal of educational practice. Specific strategies for achieving equality and for combating racism need to be developed across a broad front of school activity. Approaches should be concerned not only with overt racialist attitudes and behaviour, but with such things as how the school counters racism through both its formal and hidden curriculum, through its responses to cultural and linguistic diversity, its staffing policies, its forms of organization, its relations with parents and the community. Effective change depends on wide discussion of the issues by teachers, who must themselves be prepared to examine and assess their own attitudes.

Chapter One examines the way in which the replacement of assimilationist by pluralist objectives has altered the policy framework within which teachers are working. A gap between policy and practice has developed and has led to approaches which argue that the prime objective should be equality and combating racism. Chapters Two and Three are primarily concerned with the ways in which schools are responding. The importance of 'whole-school' approaches is emphasized, and the need to provide effective support for teachers. Chapter Four considers the way in which the education system has reacted to minority ethnic groups' particular needs and argues that effective positive action programmes are required. The position of bilingual and bidialectal pupils is then looked at in Chapter Five; this provides an example of the way in which response to diversity is leading to positive reappraisals of general educational practice which benefit all children. There is then a short concluding section.

Chapter One

Policy, practice and new approaches

At the level of official policy significant changes have taken place in educational response to ethnic diversity. Initial assimilationist objectives have been replaced by pluralist aims. Early preoccupation with helping newcomers to adapt has widened into consideration of the implications for the education system as a whole of the presence of minority ethnic groups. But there has been much less progress in giving the altered objectives practical effect. Little concerted effort has been directed towards bringing about change, and a widening gap has opened up between stated policies and practice in most educational institutions.

A time lag between the development of educational theory and its implementation is to be expected. But in this case there are more complex reasons for the gulf between official rhetoric and classroom practice. Advocacy of tolerance and harmony in response to cultural difference is a relatively simple matter if confined to vague exhortation – especially when abstracted from the realities of racial discrimination and prejudice. But once attention is turned to securing equality, and to the factors which prevent equality, the task facing the education system at once assumes greater and more complex proportions. A comprehensive review of the attitudes and assumptions which underlie existing teaching is necessary; 'multi-cultural education' cannot simply be grafted on as an exotic addition to an established curriculum. Systematic consideration of the pervasive effects of past and present racism must, for example, be integral to the process. It is easy to incorporate pluralist aims into official rhetoric but difficult to implement them in classrooms. Teachers developing approaches in schools are finding that what is involved is more complex than the vague and uncontentious language of official policy often suggests.

To understand the issues now being discussed in schools and the nature of the difficult decisions facing teachers, it is necessary to look at the way in which official policies have developed. These policies have established the framework within which teachers are now working. The first part of this chapter considers the nature and effects of racism and the overall context created by government race relations policies. The second section then examines the development of official educational policies. The shift from assimilationist to pluralist objectives is considered, and the way in which a widening gap between policy and practice has led to the development of new approaches which emphasize equality and the central importance of combating racism.

Racism and race relations

Early Government responses

Considerable criticism has been levelled against successive British governments of the 1950s and early 1960s on the grounds that during the early stages of immigration there was no policy on the implications for society of the presence of the newcomers. Black immigration into Britain chiefly took place at a time when the economic boom following the period of post-war austerity had created a situation in which an expanding economy was actively recruiting labour. Immigrants came initially predominantly from the West Indies and then from India, from 1955, and from Pakistan, from 1957, to fill jobs in Britain where there was a labour shortage. There were policy assumptions relating to the presence of these new immigrants, as Rose, in particular, has shown, but these led very largely to a policy of inaction (Rose *et al.*, 1969).

The distinction is important because reluctance to take positive action – particularly in the field of social policy – became a recurrent feature of much of the subsequent response. The attitude was that citizens were to be treated equally before the law; but the corollary was that equal treatment meant the same treatment and that no further action was necessary. In practice, it fell largely to voluntary unofficial agencies to fill the policy vacuum as best they could. Such early initiatives as there were were made in response to immediate welfare needs. In effect, immigrants were firmly categorized as strangers facing problems, not as citizens suffering disadvantage and exposed to racial discrimination. The principle of civil rights before the law was not considered to extend to the notion that the law might also guarantee social rights through legislation against discrimination.

The underlying assumption implicit in this early approach was that immigrants would be assimilated into existing British society – as earlier immigrants had largely been. The policy was rarely expressed in such extreme terms as those used by the Royal Commission on Population in 1949 when it declared that migrants could only be welcomed 'without reserve' if they were 'not prevented by their religion from intermarrying with the host population and becoming merged in it', but throughout this period the policy approach was that the newcomers would eventually simply be absorbed into British society (HMSO, 1949). This was the emphasis, for example, in the terms of reference of the Commonwealth Immigrants Advisory Council set up in 1962 'to assist immigrants to adapt themselves to British habits and customs'.

Immigration control

The 1960s saw a change of emphasis. Against a background of mounting evidence of racial discrimination in society successive governments were drawn into a more interventionist role and embarked on what developed into the twin – and contradictory – major political responses to a multi-racial Britain. These policies were immigration control and anti-discrimination legislation. Under the 1948 Nationality Act immigrants from the Commonwealth were accorded full citizenship rights, but these were subsequently steadily eroded. The Immigration Acts of 1962, 1968 and 1971, based on colour consciousness, successively and disproportionately limited black immigration. In 1981 a new Nationality Act became law which created a hierarchy of citizenship which discriminated against those from the 'New Commonwealth'. The spirit and effect of these measures was in direct contradiction to the principle of 'racial equality' concurrently being propounded. The then leader of the ILEA, Davis, commenting on the 1981 Nationality Act, told the Home Secretary that

> Not only will it affect the particular children involved but it will make it more difficult to develop in our education service the understanding necessary to provide an education which has the confidence of the people of Inner London. (Davis, 1981)

The context created by the Immigration and Nationality Acts inevitably weakened the positive element in the government's strategy – the Race Relations Acts of 1965, 1968 and 1976 which introduced increasingly strengthened legislation against racial discrimination. These departures from the studied inaction of the 1950s were accompanied by a redefinition of aims. In 1966 the then Home Secretary, Roy Jenkins, declared that the objective was 'integration' which he defined as 'not a flattening process of assimilation but as equal opportunity accompanied by cultural diversity in an atmosphere of mutual tolerance'. It is this broad – and vague – definition of a 'multi-cultural society' which has since been reiterated.

Racial discrimination

A mounting body of evidence has detailed the extent to which the 'equal opportunity' called for by the Home Secretary in 1966 – the necessary prerequisite for positive response to cultural diversity – is negated by the persistent and damaging effects of racism. The most comprehensive picture of the way this operates in Britain is contained in the findings of a research project carried out by Political and Economic Planning between 1972 and 1975 (Smith, 1977). This study demonstrated beyond argument the existence of discrimination by race in many areas of life, especially employment and housing. Blacks were found to be more vulnerable to unemployment than whites; they were concentrated within lower job levels in a way which could not be explained by lower academic or job qualifications and within broad categories of jobs they had lower earnings than whites, particularly at the higher end of the job scale. An analysis of the patterns of employment suggested that discrimination was an important factor in the disadvantaged employment position of blacks and case studies confirmed this. In controlled experiments of job applications for white-collar jobs, for example, Asian and West Indian applicants faced discrimination in 30 per cent of cases and in applications for unskilled jobs in 46 per cent of cases.

Comparable patterns of discrimination were shown to operate in housing. Owner occupation, while high for ethnic minorities, had none of the connotations of wealth which it had for the white population. The property involved was of low quality and unlikely to constitute a means of transferring wealth between generations. All the measures of housing quality used in the survey showed ethnic minorities to be much worse housed than whites. Black private tenants were paying much higher rents than white tenants, and ethnic minorities were found to be under-represented in council housing as a whole while startlingly over-represented in the lowest-quality housing. In another study, Rutter and Madge carried out an extensive review of the literature on deprivation generally and concluded that much of the future of ethnic minorities depended on the extent to which they were placed in a disadvantaged position through discriminatory practices: 'Although there are specific issues which arise from immigration and from differences in cultural background, to a large extent the "colour problem" is the problem of white racism' (Rutter and Madge, 1976).

Racial attacks

In an extreme form racial prejudice is also manifest in direct racial attacks. Racial violence against black people is little documented and receives little coverage in the national or local media. But it is much more extensive than is commonly realized. One official source – a 1981 Home Office Report on Racial Attacks – showed that the rate of racial victimization 'for Asians [was] 50 times that for white people and the rate for blacks [West Indians] was over 36 times that for white people' (HMSO 1981a). Moreover, the study found that many incidents of racial attacks were not reported to the police and that 'the results presented represent only a proportion – probably a small proportion – of the number that take place'. The report acknowledged that 'the problem has deteriorated significantly within the space of the last year'. The level of attacks appeared to be on the increase. The Home Office study – hardly a document to dramatize the seriousness of the situation – reported that 'In some places there was a sense of uncomplaining acceptance among some Asians to manifestations of racial violence; the problem was thought to be so widespread that they regarded it as little more than an unwelcome feature of contemporary British life.' The report also found evidence that 'racialist activity in schools is increasing'.

Race relations legislation

When looked at in terms of the documented extent and effect of racism government incursions into race relations legislation appear belated, hesitant and largely ineffectual. Initial approaches were marked by extreme caution. The first piece of legislation, the 1965 Race Relations Act, was limited in scope and the Race Relations Board set up under it operated conciliation procedures which were cumbersome and ineffective. In 1968 a second Act extended the grounds on which complaints of discrimination could be referred to the Race Relations Board and set up a new promotional agency, the Community Relations Commission, to encourage 'harmonious community relations'. The emphasis remained firmly on caution, conciliation and persuasion. The motivating concern of both Acts was the avoidance of racial strife rather than the provision of effective legal redress for citizens suffering from discrimination.

By the mid-1970s official policy conceded that racism was more widespread and intractable than had previously been acknowledged. A government White Paper published in 1975, after a year-long review of race relations, concluded that experience was showing that

> early optimism may not be justified, that the problems with which we have to deal if we are to see genuine equality of opportunity for the coloured youngsters born and educated in this country may be larger in scale and more complex than had been initially supposed. (HMSO, 1975)

The result was fresh legislation. The 1976 Race Relations Act adopted a new approach. This time an attempt was made to deal with discrimination not only in terms of intentional individual acts – direct injuries done by one person against another – but also with discriminatory effects. A widened definition of discrimination – treating another person less favourably because of colour, race, ethnic or national origins – was now allied to the concept of 'indirect' discrimination – the application of conditions that cannot be justified on non-racial grounds but which affect unequally particular groups. The new agency set up under the Act, the Commission for Racial Equality, was given new powers of investigation and was enpowered to call for documents and witnesses and to issue non-discrimination notices.

But despite its new powers, the Commission for Racial Equality, like its predecessors, has made limited impact. It has found the mounting of formal investigations expensive and slow, and has tended to become bogged down in casework. The Commission's first chairman, David Lane (a former Conservative MP and Home Office Minister) argued that the law needed to be strengthened if the Commission was to be effective. But this has not happened. In 1982, Lane warned that 'all recent research has shown the persistence of racial discrimination on a serious scale' and that continuing economic recession could only make things worse (Lane, 1982). In one such piece of research Little and Robbins, in a study of transmitted deprivation, found that not only were ethnic minorities disproportionately experiencing 'the worst that our society has to offer' but that 'this is continuing through to second and subsequent generations with consequences for society as a whole which are no longer potentially serious but actually so' (Little and Robbins, 1982).

Social policy

Government has accepted – in theory – that an attack on the

causes of discrimination needs to be accompanied by action to counter its deep-rooted effects. The 1975 White Paper which preceded the 1976 Race Relations Act recognized that use of the law against racial discrimination, on which government had largely relied for the previous decade, would have limited results if unaccompanied by a concerted social policy response. The White Paper argued for a 'fuller strategy'; 'a more comprehensive structure' was necessary to combat 'a cumulative cycle of disadvantage' exacerbated by racial discrimination whereby 'an entire group of people are launched on a vicious downward spiral of deprivation' (HMSO, 1975). But this theoretical analysis has not been given practical effect. When, in the summer of 1981, disturbances on the streets of Bristol, Brixton in London and Toxteth in Liverpool gave more ominous warning of the effects of continued neglect, the official inquiry conducted by Lord Scarman came to conclusions which echoed those of the Government White Paper six years earlier. 'Racial disadvantage is a fact of current British life ... urgent action is needed if it is not to become an endemic, ineradicable disease threatening the very survival of our society' (Scarman, 1981). Some thirty years after the first substantial migration from the West Indies effective policies for Britain's multi-racial society still remain, in the 1975 White Paper's phrase, to be 'worked out'.

Education policies

The development of education policy has in many ways reflected the pattern of overall government race relations policy. The DES has consistently been reluctant to take a strong lead and has tended to react to developments, often belatedly and largely ineffectually, rather than initiate positive policies. This has led to a wide variety of uneven responses by local education authorities (LEAs). The consequence of lack of central leadership and guidance has not simply been action or inaction at local level. Some of the developments which have taken place, particularly those which have been preoccupied with exotic aspects of cultural difference and have ignored the effects of racism, are now argued to have had unintended negative consequences.

Early responses: the 'problem of' immigrants

Early educational responses were dominated by a largely *ad hoc* approach to the 'problems' created by the presence of minority ethnic group pupils. The educational task was seen by the DES as the 'successful assimilation of immigrant children' (DES, 1963). It was hoped that this could be accomplished with minimum disruption to the school system. By 1965 the Department was worried that 'As the proportion of immigrant children increases, the problems will become more difficult to solve, and the chances of assimilation more remote' (DES, 1965). The answer was to recommend to LEAs that they disperse immigrant pupils, although in the event most authorities chose to ignore this advice. At a time of increasing consciousness of negative racial attitudes among the white majority – this was the year in which the first Race Relations Act was introduced – the Department was looking over its shoulder at the response of white parents and the spectre of the 'white backlash'.

A sentence printed in italics in the 1965 DES Circular was symptomatic of early attitudes; it warned

> It will be helpful if the parents of non-immigrant children can see that practical measures have been taken to deal with the problems in the schools, and that the progress of their own children is not being restricted by the undue preoccupation of the teaching staff with the linguistic and other difficulties of the immigrant children.

Immigrants *per se* were being identified as constituting a problem. This has been a recurrent feature of much discussion of education and race; there is a common tendency to allow what Green has described as 'that critical slippage from "the problems encountered by" to the "problem of"' (Green, 1982).

Lack of central leadership

During the 1960s, working within a broadly assimilationist policy frame, the emphasis was on helping minority ethnic group children to adapt to British schools. In practice, this was largely confined to teaching English as a second language. The DES offered spasmodic advice, and, from 1965, some measure of extra funding was available for multi-racial schools. But the methods adopted for administering these resources did not enable the DES either to initiate action at local level or to monitor response (see Chapter Four). Two reports in the early 1970s drew attention to the consequences. A research study showed that appropriate LEA provision was patchy and uneven (Townsend, 1971; Townsend and Brittan, 1972) and a Parliamentary Select Committee Report criticized the DES for not developing a concerted strategy and providing adequate resources to fund it (HMSO, 1973). One of the Select Committee's recommendations was that a special fund should be set up and that a condition for using it should be that authorities make full reports to central government on provision and strategies in their areas. But the DES was – and has largely remained – reluctant to adopt a positive interventionist role of this kind. The proposal was rejected on the grounds that it might 'reduce the scope of local responsibility' (HMSO, 1974). When a second large-scale survey of LEA provision was carried out in 1980, it found that the wide variations both in the scale and quality of services, reported ten years earlier, still largely persisted (Little and Willey, 1981 and 1983). In part, this reflects varying local situations and differing priorities within a decentralized education system. But primarily it is a result of the 'benign neglect' with which the DES has left the complexities of responding to ethnic diversity to be confronted at local level. It is partly because of this that when 'multi-cultural' objectives were adopted they made little impact on educational practice.

'Multi-cultural' objectives

During the 1970s pluralist objectives replaced policies of assimilation within a number of national education systems. In Britain the DES began referring to 'this country's multi-cultural society' and argued that this should be reflected in teaching in all schools. By the time the 'great debate' on the curriculum got under way at the end of the decade this view had assumed a central place in DES publications. For example, the Department's important 1981 paper on *The School Curriculum* – the result of 'several years of public discussion and Government consultation with its education partners' – was categoric about the extent to which teaching in all schools should reflect the changed ethnic composition of society:

> What is taught in schools, and the way it is taught, must appropriately reflect fundamental values in our society ... the work of schools has to reflect many issues with which pupils will have to come to terms as they mature, and schools and teachers are familiar with them. First, our society has become multi-cultural; and there is now among pupils and parents a greater diversity of personal values. (DES, 1981a)

Closely comparable radical changes in direction at the level of theoretical policy took place in Australia and Canada. In Australia in 1966 the Minister of Immigration was explicit that the then prevailing aim was assimilation: 'We must have a single culture ... we should have a mono-culture, with everyone living in the same way, understanding each other, and sharing the same aspirations' (Cigler, 1975). But four years later, his successor announced a change in policy. He stated that 'The earlier desire to make stereotype Australians of the newcomers has been cast aside' (Lynch, 1972). In 1975 the Australian Schools Commission was spelling out the educational implications; it urged that where groups 'have a distinctive culture of their own, as do ethnic minorities, it should be sustained and other groups encouraged to recognise its authenticity' (Australian Schools Commission, 1975). In 1981 when the Curriculum Development Centre in Canberra published its *Core Curriculum for Australian Schools*, pluralist aims had assumed a central place in directly the same way in which they had in Britain (Curriculum Development Centre, 1980). 'The multi-cultural composition and interest of our population' appeared as one of a number of changes in Australian society which, it was argued, all schools must respond to. Among the list of 'fundamental learning for all students' were included:

> Focus on general, universal elements in culture for present and future life, i.e. the common culture; acknowledge the plural, multi-cultural nature of our society and seek a form of cultural-social integration which values interaction and free communication amongst diverse groups and sub-groups, i.e. the common multi-culture.

In Canada up until the end of the 1960s 'Anglo-conformity' had been based on 'the desirability of sustaining British institutions and norms as the established basis for building Canadian society' (Palmer and Tropper, 1973). But in 1971 the Prime Minister announced a new departure into 'multi-cultural' policies predicated on 'assuring the cultural freedom of all Canadians'. In 1972 a Minister of State responsible for Multi-culturalism was appointed, and a special Directorate was established to increase among 'society at large... awareness and appreciation of the bi-lingual and multi-cultural nature of our country'. By 1976 the Toronto Board of Education was declaring that 'If we are to appreciate differences and commonalities multi-cultural education must be a basis for our school system and must be directed to all students and teachers' (Toronto Board of Education, 1976).

The implications for teachers

The implications for teachers of these changes in policy assumptions are very considerable. Over a relatively short period response to ethnic diversity has ceased to be seen as the responsibility of a small number of English as a second language (E2L) specialists who would prepare children for life in mainstream schools, and has become something which – so official policy now argues – has consequences for all teachers in all schools. In 1979, Bolton, at the time a senior HM Inspector with responsibilities in this field, was arguing in relation to Britain that the two issues of the nature of educational provision in multi-racial schools and the nature of provision for all pupils in a pluralist society were not only 'inter-related but inter-dependent' (Bolton, 1979).

If these newly promulgated objectives for all schools were to make serious impact, specific and concerted action would be necessary to bring about change – to counteract what Casso has characterized in relation to the United States, for example, as 'a 200-year old history of a monolingual, monocultural and ethnocentric thrust in the public schools' (Casso, 1976). Wide consideration of the issues raised would have to be generated within schools and throughout the education service. There would need to be a significant input into in-service training programmes and into the initial training of new teachers. Detailed work on considering such things as the implications for different areas of the curriculum would have to be initiated. But in practice within the education systems of Britain, Australia, Canada and the United States such developments have either been on a limited and ineffective scale or have been non-existent. Broad policy objectives have been propounded but implementation has largely been left to vague exhortation not systematic action to secure educational change.

Neglect of racism

Above all, 'multi-cultural' policies have uniformly failed to address the central influence of racism. The context in which teachers are being asked to develop pluralist approaches is one in which, as has been shown earlier in this chapter, the effect of racism is well documented. The deeply damaging conse-quences for society have been acknowledged. The British government's 1975 White Paper, referred to earlier, accepted that 'It is the Government's duty to prevent morally unaccept-able and socially divisive inequalities from hardening into entrenched patterns' and went on

> It is inconceivable that Britain in the last quarter of the Twentieth Century should confess herself unable to secure for a small minority of around a million and a half coloured citizens their full and equal rights as individual men and women (HMSO, 1975).

But the everyday experience of teachers – and of both their black and white pupils – is that the 'inconceivable' is continuing to happen. Racism is an inescapable element in the life of the societies now developing pluralist objectives. At school level, teachers are well aware of this and are increas-ingly arguing that response to prejudice has to be made explicit in formal school policies, in dealing with overt racialist behaviour, in the curriculum, in teaching materials, in forms of school organization, in self-examination by teachers of their own attitudes.

A gap between policy and practice

The failure of 'multi-cultural' objectives to combat racism and the failure to adopt serious strategies to bring about educa-tional change have resulted in a wide gap between official theory and educational practice. This is apparent at two levels. In predominantly all-white schools, pluralist aims have made virtually no impact at all. In multi-racial schools developments have often been preoccupied with cultural differences; approaches have generally remained marginal to the major concerns of the curriculum and pupils' awareness of the realities of black-white relations in society has been little affected.

In Britain a survey in 1980 of all LEAs and of 300 secondary schools with few or no pupils from minority ethnic groups (under 2½ per cent) found that official assertions about a 'multi-cultural' society having relevance to all schools had made minimal impact (Little and Willey, 1981). Most authorities with few minority ethnic group pupils commented that 'multi-cultural education' was not a matter which concerned them, and that it would in any case have very low priority as against more pressing calls on their time and energies. These authorities considered that if there was a need to take action they would hear about it from the schools, but that to take any kind of positive initiative themselves would only be divisive and would generate hostility. The great majority of head teachers expressed similar views. Typical written comments from head teachers in reply to a question-naire were:

Presumably minority ethnic groups are here because they wish to be – why should it then be incumbent upon the indigenous population to change?

In my opinion far too much time, energy and money is devoted to a very small minority in this country ... regardless of colour or creed anyone who wishes to come and settle should adapt to the British way of life and all that this implies, rather than the other way round.

I believe the emphasis should be on similarities not differences. To draw attention to racial minorities, far from being helpful, only tends to hinder assimilation and make people conscious of 'non-existent' problems.

The same survey found that although significant initiatives had been taken in some multi-racial LEAs, in practice overall provision continued to be overwhelmingly preoccupied with meeting the basic language needs of E2L learners. Important innovations had taken place in a minority of multi-racial schools; these are considered in Chapters Two and Three. But, generally, developments had been limited in scope and remained peripheral to the main concerns of schools. Another survey, of in-service provision, concluded that there was 'no doubt about the fragmentary and incomplete provision of in-service teacher education for a multi-cultural society. Indeed, it is non-existent in many areas and in none is it wholly adequate' (Eggleston, Dunn and Purewall, 1981). A number of other reports and surveys in the early 1980s reached similar conclusions, notably a report from the Parliamentary Home Affairs Committee on *Racial Disadvantage* (HMSO, 1981b). In 1980 the DES appointed a special Committee of Inquiry into the Education of Children from Ethnic Minority Groups which published an Interim Report (the Rampton Report: Rampton, 1981a). The Committee argued that urgent and wide-ranging initiatives were needed if schools were to respond effectively to West Indian pupils (see below, Chapter Four).

A similar situation prevails in other countries. In Canada a number of studies have documented a 'disheartening gap between the policies … and the realities' (Deosaran, 1977; Ghosh, 1978; Samuda, 1980). The Multi-cultural Directorate has made little impact on education; as Bhatnagar and Hamalian summarize the position 'there seems little doubt that the concept of multi-culturalism has neither affected educational policy making at the school level nor the educational practice of a very large body of teachers' (Bhatnagar and Hamalian, 1981). A survey of schools in Ontario found that 'in classroom after classroom' minority ethnic groups were 'being subjected … to continued programmes of Canadianization based on the concept of and belief in assimilation' (McLeod, 1975). In Australia, the position is much the same; for example, an Australian Department of Education report on schools of 'high migrant density' in New South Wales and Victoria found that 'most of the schools continued to function in a "narrow" assimilationist mould' (Australian Department of Education, 1975). In the United States a branch was set up within the Federal Office of Education nominally to implement the Title IX legislation referred to in the Introduction, but its funding allocation ($2.3 million in 1978) and its effect have been minimal. When practical response was required to the 150,000 Vietnamese who entered America in 1975, Kelly has shown that a strongly assimilationist approach was adopted which made no concessions to pluralist ideology (Kelly, 1981).

Criticisms of 'multi-cultural' approaches

The failure of educational policy makers to address the realities of racism has led some educationalists – many of them black – to question the relevance and validity of 'multi-cultural' objectives altogether. These writers argue that preoccupation with cultural difference deflects from the real issues affecting the education of black children. Official policies are seen at best as largely irrelevant and ineffectual, and at worst as positively harmful or primarily about social control.

Carby, for example, suggests that

> The paradigm of multi-culturalism actually excludes the concept of dominant and subordinate cultures – either indigenous or migrant – and fails to recognise that the existence of racism relates to the possession and exercise of politico-economic control and authority and also to forms of resistance to the power of dominant social groups. (Carby, 1980)

For Mullard multi-culturalism 'is none other than a more sophisticated form of social control and it has the effect of containing black resistance' (Mullard, 1981). Dhondy argues a similar thesis: the development of 'multi-cultural' objectives by the educational establishment has been a conscious strategy to contain the challenge presented by disaffected black youth (Dhondy, 1978). Verma and Bagley argue that many black pupils who react against the system do so because of the effects of racism:

> The rebellion of black students in British schools is sometimes classed in pathological terms, as behaviour disorders. We believe, however, that this reaction to the alienating forces of the school may often, perhaps very often, be a form of rebellion by black students attempting to establish a meaningful form of identity based on a resistance to the alienating forces in school and society. (Verma and Bagley, 1979)

Stone has mounted a powerful critique of multi-cultural approaches from a somewhat different standpoint. She charges the education system with failing to educate black pupils. The introduction of 'multi-cultural' elements into the teaching of black children is an irrelevance based on the erroneous view that black children have a poor self image, and it deflects from the need to teach normal basic skills effectively. The prevailing reality of 'multi-cultural' education – based mainly on steel bands, participation in sport and Black Studies – thus adversely affects the education of black children, it is 'a misguided liberal strategy to compensate black children for not being white' (Stone, 1981).

Similar criticisms have been advanced in other countries. In America there was heated debate in the 1960s over the introduction of approaches such as Black Studies, Chicano Studies and Judaic Studies. Reaction against these developments was expressed in very similar terms to those advanced by Stone in Britain, as the title of a 1969 article in the *New York Times* by a black educator indicates: 'The Road to the Top is through Higher Education – not Black Studies' (Lewis, 1969).

The argument was that good teaching of basic skills was needed, not the romanticizing of 'quaint cultural heritages with little value to the labour market' (Killian, 1983). In Canada, Davis has argued – in terms similar to those applied by Mullard to the UK – that official multi-cultural policies are 'a means of "containing" the demands of ethnic minorities without envisaging basic changes in the power structure of Canadian society' (Davis, 1975). As Wilson sees it:

> The Canadian multi-culturalism policy seems to guarantee that we can each do our little dances and flash our pretty, lacy petticoats while we drink our ethnic drinks and admire each other's handicrafts … it does not speak to the injustice that pervades our daily lives if our hair or skin colour is unlike that of the members at the top of the column (Wilson, 1978).

Defining pluralist aims in schools

These brief extracts from some of the main contributors to the debate give an indication of the powerful critique which has been mounted against official 'multi-cultural' approaches. The arguments are particularly persuasive because the failure to develop strategies for applying pluralist aims to classroom practice has meant that, whatever the theoretical policies, change in schools has been minimal. But as Green has pointed out in relation to Britain, in an important rejoinder to some of the writers quoted above,

> multi-cultural education barely yet exists in our schools … rather than talk about multi-cultural education as an accomplished fact, we should think in terms of an agenda of reforms which have been collectively called multi-culturalism and a struggle which is being waged on the grounds marked out by this agenda. (Green, 1982)

It is in classrooms that the real issues and complexities of responding positively to ethnic diversity in society are emerging and are being confronted constructively. It is the staff of multi-racial schools who – often collectively – are defining and beginning to implement pluralist developments in education. In these schools what Green calls 'an interventionist approach' is being adopted, the key to which is not simply passively reflecting diversity, but engaging positively and decisively with racism. The ways in which this is happening in schools is examined in the next two chapters.

New approaches

In Britain the weakness of previous 'multi-cultural' approaches has led to the development of new policy perspectives which emphasize equality. These policies have resulted from closely related initiatives in two LEAs, Berkshire and the ILEA. The hitherto adopted perspective 'emphasising mainly Cultural Diversity' is criticized on five main grounds (ILEA, 1983b):

  (i) Its almost exclusive emphasis on aspects of culture and cultural differences tends to obscure or ignore other issues: the economic position of black people in relation to white people; differences in access to resources and in power to affect events; discrimination in employment, housing, and education; relations with the police.

 (ii) It conceives of racism as merely a set of mental prejudices held by a smallish number of unenlightened white people, and hence ignores or denies the structural aspects of racism, both in the education system and in society.

(iii) It reflects a white view of black cultures as homogeneous, static, conflict-free, exotic. It ignores the power relations between white and black people, both in history and in the present.

(iv) It ignores the issue which black people themselves consider to be of vital importance – that is, the issue of racism and the promotion of racial equality.

(v) Although it recognises the right of people to maintain their own cultures, in practice this is limited to support for marginal activities, which do not impinge on mainstream social policies and programmes.

For these reasons it is argued that a perspective emphasizing diversity and pluralism must be included in a context which addresses issues of racism and its effects on both black and white people. This new policy approach continues to stress the importance of positive responses to cultural and linguistic diversity. But a significantly different approach is applied. The focus is on equality, and also on racism. As Sivanandan argues, the central concern must be with

anti-racist education (which by its very nature would include the study of other cultures). Just to learn about other people's cultures, though, is not to learn about the racism of one's own. To learn about the racism of one's own culture, on the other hand, is to approach other cultures objectively. (Sivanandan, 1982)

The policy statement adopted by Berkshire LEA (1983a) clearly demonstrates the important departure from the vague concerns of the official 'multi-cultural' objectives discussed earlier in this chapter. The authority's policy

requires and supports all its educational institutions and services to create, maintain and promote racial equality and justice.

The Council is opposed to racism in all its forms. It wishes therefore:-

1 To promote understanding of the principles and practices of racial equality and justice, and commitment to them.

2 To identify and remove all practices, procedures and customs which discriminate against ethnic minority people and to replace them with procedures which are fair to all.

3 To encourage ethnic minority parents and communities to be fully involved in the decision-making processes which affect the education of their children.

4 To increase the influence of ethnic minority parents, organisations and communities by supporting educational and cultural projects which they themselves initiate.

5 To encourage the recruitment of echnic minority teachers, administrators and other staff at all levels, and the appointment of ethnic minority governors.

6 To monitor and evaluate the implementation of (LEA) policies, and to make changes and corrections as appropriate.

The remainder of this book is primarily concerned with ways in which such aims can be put into educational practice.

SUMMARY

This chapter has argued that the pervasive effects of racism are deeply entrenched in society. The consequences have been acknowledged in official rhetoric, but not in terms of an effective policy response. In education there has been a radical shift in theoretical objectives from assimilation to pluralism. A major consequence is that responding to ethnic diversity is a concern of all teachers, regardless of the particular ethnic composition of the school in which they work. But strategies have not been developed to implement the new objectives and a gap has opened up between policy and practice. Most importantly, the theoretical 'multi-cultural' objectives have failed to address the central question of racism. Schools cannot respond to ethnic and cultural diversity without confronting the realities of prejudice and discrimination. This has led to the development of new policy approaches which emphasize equality and justice.

Chapter Two

Racism and schools

In multi-racial schools the discrepancy between official policies and classroom realities can appear acute. The DES sees 'multi-cultural' approaches creating in schools 'a microcosm of a happy and co-operative world'. Teachers are often faced by racist abuse and bullying and the dissemination of racist literature. Some schools have found it necessary to organize escort rotas to protect black children on their way home. In such schools it is being recognized that explicitly countering racism must be a prerequisite for developing positive responses to ethnic and cultural diversity. At one level this involves implementing policies to deal with overt prejudiced behaviour. But it also means systematically examining the ways in which institutionalized racism may operate through the procedures and practices of the school.

This chapter looks at the ways in which responses to racism

are now emerging. How are policies being developed? What do they comprise? How are they being implemented? Schools have to counter racism through the formal and hidden curriculum, through approaches to cultural and linguistic diversity, through staffing policies, forms of organization, relations with parents and the community. Newly developing approaches have comprehensive implications for many aspects of school life and examples are given of the ways in which teachers are responding in a range of different areas of educational activity. Many of the innovative developments taking place in multi-racial schools are equally relevant to all-white schools. As with so many aspects of responding to ethnic diversity, it is in multi-racial schools that the issues are most apparent but they have direct relevance to the provision of good education generally.

'Colour-blind' or anti-racist?

In 1982 a London head teacher characterized the choice facing teachers as being:

> do we ignore the problems of racism and racialist organisations and hope they will disappear? Or do we, as a multi-racial school, take a principled stand against them. The same dilemma presented itself to the German people in the early 1930s and they took the former course with disastrous consequences. We cannot afford the same mistakes. (ILEA, 1982a)

The warning was provoked by the wide reluctance in the education system over the previous decades to intervene positively in what was regarded as the dangerous and contentious field of race relations. Many schools adopted a 'colour-blind' approach – 'We have no problems here. We treat all children as children.' Good race relations could best be secured through stealth rather than potentially provocative direct action. To draw attention to inequalities would be to invite trouble. Wilson reports the following 'well meaning and typical' response from a junior school head when questioned about racial remarks in her school:

> Asking them to say 'thank you' and 'please' or asking them not to swear is one thing but asking them not to say 'nigger' or 'wog' or 'black people stink' is quite another. A discussion of these things would only make matters worse. (Wilson, 1983)

Many heads of multi-racial secondary schools who returned written questionnaires to a Schools Council survey in 1980 reported views which, although expressed less forthrightly, amounted to a similar approach:

> A teacher teaches all children in the class and is not concerned with race, creed or colour; pupils are pupils of the school regardless of ethnic background.

> I feel the more one goes out of one's way to teach about racialism the more one is in danger of creating the problem one is setting out to cure.

> We regard children as children not as members of ethnic groups.

> I am concerned that we should not exacerbate or even manufacture problems by tactlessly fussing about our multi-ethnic situation …. If we try to be too dogmatic we risk polarising the racial groups with very unpleasant results.

> I consider the absurd pathological preoccupation with race is becoming divisive of our cohesive society.

> The less emphasis on this matter the more harmonious the solution. (Little and Willey, 1983)

Such views reflect central government's own cautious and hesitant approach to race relations legislation – certainly until the introduction of the 1976 Race Relations Act. They are also symptomatic of the DES's consistent inexplicitness in relation to race. It is this deeply entrenched legacy which is now being challenged.

Policy pronouncements

Although the DES has given no direct guidance on responding to racism there has been growing recognition elsewhere in the education system that explicit policies are necessary. The National Union of Teachers (NUT), for example, in 1981 published a pamphlet on *Combating Racialism in Schools*. This argued that 'it should now be clear to all teachers that ignoring racialism will not make it go away, nor will a "colour-blind" approach best serve the interests of ethnic minority pupils'. The Union recommended that staff of schools 'meet together to determine a school policy on racialism' (NUT, 1981). In 1981 a Parliamentary Select Committee urged that 'each local education authority should consider the extent to which both the hidden and formal curriculum in schools are able to combat racism by promoting equality of opportunity among all sections of the population in a multi-racial society' (HMSO, 1981c).

There have also been developments at LEA level. The 1976 Race Relations Act laid on local authorities (in Section 71) a twofold duty in the services which they provide – to eliminate unlawful racial discrimination and to promote equality of opportunity and good relations between persons of different racial groups. By 1983 some twenty LEAs had published statements, position papers or discussion documents on multi-racial education, and compliance with the Race Relations Act features prominently as a reason for policy development. But, as with the advocacy of pluralist policies at national level described in Chapter One, these LEA policies are almost exclusively concerned with responding to diversity rather than with combating racism. Dorn, in analysing LEA policies, found that the most striking feature in terms of what is not discussed is the almost total absence of any consideration of education as a system whose routine practices might be forms of institutionalized racism based on taken-for-granted assumptions rather than overt prejudices. When racism is mentioned response is at the level of a statement of intent rather than a programme of action (Dorn, 1983).

Programmes of action

In a small number of LEAs more specific and direct approaches have been adopted. The Inner London Education Authority (ILEA) provides the most striking example. In 1982 the then Chief Education Officer, Newsam, told teachers that each school in the authority should have a

> clear view, agreed within itself, on how to deal with discriminatory practices wherever they may show themselves. The obligation is plain. The education service must concern itself with everyone in this city, every child and every parent of every child must know where we stand. Whatever its source, wherever it lies, however it manifests itself, the education service is flatly opposed to racial discrimination. (ILEA, 1982a)

In 1983 the ILEA published an 'Anti-racist statement' which committed the authority 'to eliminating racism and to take such action as it properly can to remedy its effects' (ILEA, 1983b). The authority asked all educational establishments, through their staff and governing or managing bodies and in association with the communities they serve to 'prepare and publicise carefully thought-out statements of their position. This must be seen as part of the Authority's legal and educational commitment'. The Authority also published detailed 'anti-racist guidelines for ILEA establishments'. These suggested that most schools and colleges that had developed policies had found it essential to follow a process which included all of the following:

1 Placing the issue firmly on the school/college agenda and making time for discussion and development.
2 Coming to grips with what racism is and its historical context.
3 Considering how racism can and does operate in the school/college's particular circumstances.
4 Analysing both directly conscious racist behaviour and what the Rampton Interim Report terms 'unconscious racism'.
5 Analysing both individual behaviour and the policies and practices of the school/college.
6 Analysing the behaviour and practices of individuals and services that impinge on the life of the school/college.
7 Drawing upon the advice and experience of others, including other schools/colleges and those with specialist knowledge and experience.

The guidelines also indicated that although each school would determine its policy in the light of its own circumstances, certain elements would be common to all. These were:

1 A clear, unambiguous statement of opposition to any form of racism or racist behaviour.
2 A firm expression of all pupils' or students' rights to the best possible education.
3 A clear indication of what is not acceptable and the procedures, including sanctions, to deal with any transgressions.
4 An explanation of the way in which the school or college intends to develop practices which both tackle racism and create educational opportunities which make for a cohesive society and a local school or college community in which diversity can flourish.
5 An outline of the measures by which developments will be monitored and evaluated.

As well as giving guidance on ways of handling overt manifestations of racialist and discriminatory behaviour the

ILEA document indicated a range of elements in the life and work of a school which can be positively employed in order to tackle racism and so improve education. These were: ethos and climate, the content and organization of the curriculum and resources, teacher knowledge and awareness, staff relationship with pupils, processes of selection and grouping, sharing knowledge and support, relationship with parents and the community, dissemination of policies, in-service training, and monitoring.

A black perspective

A key element in the ILEA policy initiative is that central importance is attached to providing a forum in which a black perspective on the education of black pupils can be voiced. The policy was developed through widespread consultation, particularly with the black communities – 'Rather than define needs on behalf of black pupils, the Authority has listened to the words of black representatives.' The policy resulted from recognition of the need for an urgent response to these 'clearly articulated needs'. Running throughout the proposals for action in schools is emphasis that initiatives must be directly informed by the experience of the people who bear the brunt of racism. This involves developing new forms of consultation at all levels of the education service. At present, many black parents have minimal contact with schools. A survey of 225 multi-racial schools found that in 70 per cent black parents were less likely than white parents to be active in forms of parental involvement in school activities (Little and Willey, 1983). This reflects the 'unintentional racism' which operates within schools and is a contributory element in failure to respond to racism. As the ILEA 'Anti-racist statement' argues: 'In structural terms, racism is represented mainly by the formula, racism = power + prejudice and discrimination. Accordingly, power and resources in the education service, as in other institutions of our society, are in the hands of white people.' In developing anti-racist approaches in schools – as at all levels of the education service – it is essential that policies are continually informed by a black perspective; this must consciously and systematically be built into schools' responses.

Experience in schools

The process of dismantling racism has to take place across a wide front of school activities. The implications for teachers are far reaching and schools are developing policy statements and practices for dealing with overt racialist behaviour, reviewing their hidden and formal curricula, examining the influence of racism on forms of organization and on teachers' own attitudes and assumptions.

Specific approaches vary considerably between schools, both in the ways in which discussion of the issues is handled and in the strategies which are adopted. Central to the process is wide debate among teachers. It is helpful to consider a particular case in detail, not because it provides a model which can be uniformly applied elsewhere, but because it gives some indication of the nature and extent of what is involved for schools. Experience in a London girls' comprehensive has been described in a fascinating account by Shallice which provides important insights into the complexities which face teachers (Shallice, 1983).

The Skinners' Company's School's policy was evolved through wide staff participation over the course of a year. The policy as eventually formally adopted stated:

> The Governors and staff of the school welcome the multi-ethnic nature of present-day British society and are wholly opposed to racism. We condemn all expressions of racist attitudes, either through remarks or conduct, and we hope that parents and pupils will think it right to adopt a similar attitude.
>
> In order to achieve racial harmony the staff follow and will continue to follow the following principles:

(a) All pupils and staff should be treated with dignity and should feel that their particular culture is valued by the school.

(b) All pupils should be given equal opportunities to develop their potential.

(c) School life should reflect the different backgrounds of the pupils.

(d) The curriculum should reflect the various cultures of Britain.

(e) There should be open discussion about living in a multi-ethnic community and this should include discussions about the causes of racism.

(f) All racial incidents and attacks whether physical or verbal should be dealt with according to the clear school policy.

(g) Distribution of racist literature and the use of school premises by racist groups will not be allowed.

The staff hope that pupils and parents will bring to their attention any racist incidents, whether they occur in or outside school, so that they can take appropriate action.

The need for an explicitly anti-racist policy arose at a specially called meeting of all staff at which the way teachers considered racism affected the running of the school was openly discussed. From this beginning a working party was set up which produced a draft policy which was then considered at a full staff conference. Shallice reports that at this conference it was the question of whether the school was racist as an institution which produced most discussion. The general feeling, although with some dissent, was that while there was no overt racism, covert and subtle racist practices did exist. Examples of these were such things as: relatively few black teachers, unawareness of pressures facing black girls outside the school, the curriculum did not adequately reflect or value cultural diversity, stereotypes and negative images of different ethnic groups in the school existed and some staff had low expectations of black pupils. The staff recognized a need to develop specific strategies to combat such 'unintentional' racist practices as well as to deal with racist incidents. The resulting policy was formally adopted by the governors and was then discussed in detail with all pupils. It was considered particularly important that all staff in the school were seen to be identified with the policy, and a pack of teaching materials was produced for staff support. Shallice reports that in the lower school, staff considered that these discussions with pupils had been of great value. In the upper school 'the most frequent responses after the sessions were that [the policy] was good and necessary and "why was it only now that the school had made this statement?" '

Shallice describes an incident which occurred at a fairly late stage during the process of formulating the Skinners' Company's School's policy 'which played a quite major catalytic role in crystallising the need for an anti-racist policy amongst sections of the staff'. It is worth quoting at length because it illustrates both the damaging effects which unintentional racism can have and the central importance of the development of corporate approaches by staff as a whole:

A teacher in the school had been teaching a second year class, and also was dealing with two other classes, providing work and support for substitute staff, as their class teachers were absent. One of these classes was doing practical work involving the use of musical instruments and when she went in halfway through the lesson to find out how they were getting on, one of the girls whom she knew well, was playing a drum. The girl was asked to stop while some more explanation was given, but she did not do so. 'In situations like this, I sometimes find it effective to make a joke to get someone to stop doing something. Because I knew this form well, I assumed the joke would have its effect and said: "Oh come on … you're not in the jungle"; no-one laughed but she did stop. It was not until the end of the lesson that I realised the full effect of the joke. The class suddenly became very aggressive towards me. When I tried to calm them down, the girl to whom I had made the comment, plus the others, stood up and told me that I had made a racist comment, and that I had only said it because the girl concerned was black.

'I asked them if they thought I was racist, to which they replied, that they did. At this point, the pips went for the end of the lesson and they left, extremely angry and upset, leaving me absolutely astonished.'

The girls immediately went to see the deputy head and the teacher independently did so, being very upset that the girls thought her to be a racist. The deputy agreed that the teacher would be taken off time-table the next morning and would be able to spend time with the girls to talk through the incident and to apologise.

'As a result of talking to these girls for 2 hours I discovered that they felt very strongly about their race, colour and identity, and that it was nothing to joke about. They talked about how many people did not really understand how they felt. They were very grateful for the opportunity to talk about this problem.' (Shallice, 1983)

The teacher involved wrote a statement for the staff and the girls also wanted to write an essay about themselves being black. The teacher's statement and the girls' essays were made available to staff to read as part of the discussions taking place on formulating the anti-racist school policy.

As Shallice emphasizes 'What was enormously impressive was the speed at which the support was provided for both staff and pupils ... the incident was known, the teacher and girls immediately going to members of staff for some form of support and help.' Because it was dealt with quickly and positively this incident presented an extremely valuable model for both staff and pupil support.

Shallice underlines throughout her account of the development of this particular school's policy that the school is one in which the staff is in general one which feels confident about raising issues. In the discussions on racism staff were prepared to talk openly about the situation in the school and were mostly aware of support from each other. Shallice comments: 'This feature of the school permitted an ease of discussion which may well be difficult in other schools.' Open, confident and sustained expression of teachers' attitudes, experiences and ideas is the key to initiating effective strategies to combat racism, and Chapter Three gives more consideration to how schools are developing 'whole-school' approaches through which this can be achieved. The remainder of this chapter looks in more detail at specific areas of school practice in which anti-racist strategies are being adopted by teachers.

Public statements and procedures for tackling racist behaviour

In direct contradiction to the 'colour-blind' and inexplicit approaches which have so often characterized vague 'multi-cultural' responses, the need publicly to assert a clear anti-racist position is increasingly being seen as fundamental. A key element in the policy being developed in one school is:

> to state clearly and unequivocally to the general community, to parents and to pupils, the school's attitude and policy towards the provision of a secure environment which encourages learning for all pupils, and to leave no doubt that racist behaviour and any attempt to harass and intimidate minority groups will not be tolerated.

It follows from such a declaration that specific procedures need to be incorporated into a school's code of practice to deal with overt racist incidents and behaviour. Experience in schools where this has been done shows the importance of securing agreement among staff to consistent and immediate responses. If racist behaviour is condoned or overlooked the effect of discrimination in the wider society is confirmed and extended for the black child, and the racist offender concludes that the staff is either intimidated or that their behaviour has implicit support. As one school policy states: 'No member of staff should ignore any form of ... racist abuse anywhere in the school.' Any significant change in a school's policy and practices requires the involvement of parents. This is particularly important in developing anti-racist policies. The effectiveness of the school's approach will be influenced by the extent to which it successfully makes its position clear to the community as a whole and – as far as is possible – canvasses support.

The kinds of racist actions which occur in schools have been summarized by the ILEA (1983b) as:

1 Physical assault against a person or group because of colour or ethnicity.
2 Derogatory name-calling, insults and racist jokes.
3 Racist graffiti or any other written insult.
4 Provocative behaviour such as wearing racist badges or insignia.
5 Bringing racist material such as leaflets, comics or magazines into school.
6 Making threats against a person or group because of colour or ethnicity.
7 Racist comment in the course of discussion in lessons.
8 Attempts to recruit other pupils and students to racist organisations and groups.

The action to be taken by teachers must be clearly laid down and adhered to. For example, in North Westminster school's policy it has been agreed that physical attacks of a racist nature or racist intimidation will result in the following steps being taken:

(a) Report to Head of School Site.
(b) Head of School Site records in serious incident book.
(c) Full report to Head Master/Mistress.
(d) Full report to parent/guardian.

(e) Support for teacher(s) concerned, and victim(s).

(f) Follow-up to prevent recurrence.

It is important for teachers to recognize that an understanding of the cause, the reason or motive for a racialist action will have a major bearing on how that action is dealt with. Another school policy, for example, sets out clear guidelines for members of staff on how to deal with 'hard core racists', 'students on the periphery' and ' "unintentional" racists'.

Experience in one London school emphasizes the importance of careful monitoring to check how far policies are having effect (*Teaching London Kids*, No. 21). A year after the policy had received unanimous support from the whole staff a new E2L teacher wrote:

> During the past week the ESL groups have been discussing 'Names'. We have been talking about the variety of names that one person may have; first names, formal and informal names, family names, nicknames, etc. This led on to a discussion of verbal abuse. The points that emerged were interesting and disturbing.
>
> All the Bengali boys agreed that there was a persistent, often daily and usually unprovoked harassment. They were called 'Paki', 'bud-bud' or 'black bastard' regularly. It happened most usually in the playground or outside the classroom before the teacher arrived or sometimes during lessons when the teacher's attention was elsewhere. The culprits were usually the same one or two pupils in each class, boys or girls. 'It happens every day. Today "you bloddy Pakis". They start hitting us.' Most of the incidents were name-calling, but some were more serious.
>
> The boys rarely told staff of these incidents. The reason they gave was that they were afraid of reprisals. Some of the younger boys go home with 4th or 5th years for protection. They clearly lack confidence in teachers' ability to deal effectively with these incidents, and in some cases gave examples of teachers ignoring name-calling.

Subsequent review of the way the anti-racist policy was working found that the incident sheets made available to all staff for reporting racist behaviour were often not used. A number of reasons emerged: the procedure was thought to be too bureaucratic – yet another form to fill in; a 'rigid' system of recording was not seen as appropriate for dealing with individual cases; some teachers were hostile to the procedure, despite having given the policy nominal support. Given the day-to-day concerns of a regular school day, recording of racist incidents may not be seen as a priority. In the light of these findings there was further discussion of the policy among all staff and two points emerged as particularly important. First, one aim of the policy was to enable systematic monitoring of the incidence of racism in the school; this depended on every incident being written up. Second, renewed emphasis was put on making the procedures public throughout the school; a major reason for introducing the policy was to make explicit to the school as a whole the teachers' complete opposition to racism and their determination to act against it.

Ethos and atmosphere

As the policy of a London comprehensive makes clear: 'Physical environment can reflect racism by graffiti in and around school premises; by lack of signs in languages other than English; and by the absence of displays reflecting a multi-cultural community' (ILEA, 1982a). Alternatively, the elements that together make up the ethos and climate of a school can give a positive message which is clearly opposed to racism. For example, assemblies and other group meetings can be used consistently to emphasize the pluralist nature of society and of the school and to underline aims of equality. Displays on walls throughout the buildings can have a similar emphasis. Public notices giving directions can be displayed in the major languages of the school community. School rules and regulations can be sensitive to, and show respect for, diverse cultural practices, such as those relating to religion, diet and dress.

Teachers are often unaware of the significance which attention even to seemingly minor details can make. Dunn quotes the experience of a teacher who, after being on an in-service course, tentatively began to put pictures of black people on the walls of her classroom:

> I found that the children did actually notice these. Children I didn't even teach used to come into the classroom to look at pictures of the Soledad brothers and sometimes they were amazed that I actually knew about these people .... Perhaps I'm making too much of this but I feel that they did recognise that I'd taken a little bit of trouble ... this was quite a big thing for some of the kids. (Dunn, 1983)

Cumulatively positive attention to such things can contribute significantly to the well-being, confidence, security and identity of all pupils and students. Consciously and systematically applied across the whole range of activities which contribute to the ethos of a school, this sort of emphasis constitutes an important element in enabling issues of racism to be raised naturally and dealt with effectively.

The curriculum

Combating racism and developing positive responses to diversity have major implications for all areas of the curriculum. The scope of what is involved is indicated by the policy of one school which states that (ILEA, 1982a):

> The curriculum, explicit and hidden, must aim, through the over-arching whole-school policies, the separate subject department syllabuses, the tutorial programme and all curriculum planning:
>
> 1 to create an understanding of and interest in different environments, societies, systems and cultures across the world;

2 to study the political, social and economic reasons for racism and equality, and their present-day effects in this country and the world;

3 to encourage pupils to recognise that each society has its own values, traditions and everyday living patterns which should be considered in the context of that society;

4 to study scientific achievements outside the western world, and alternative approaches to science;

5 to explore and share the ideas, opinions and interests which derive from particular cultural experience. Its content should be so selected that it engages pupils' feelings as well as giving them skills and information;

6 to develop the concepts and skills which will allow pupils to criticise and actively participate in all social institutions, e.g. media, political parties, etc.

Consideration of how teachers are approaching the extensive and complex task indicated by this sort of analysis of what is required is undertaken in the next chapter. But, in general terms, it is important to emphasize that, because of the entrenched nature of racist influences, examination of the implications of the operation of past and present racism for the curriculum must be set in a wide historical frame. It has been argued that the historical conditions which lie behind present black–white relations – colonial exploitation and repression, slavery, massive and sustained discrimination by white society against black people – have resulted in 'a kind of historical amnesia, a decisive mental repression, which has overtaken the British people about race and Empire since the 1950s' and has led to an attempt to blot out the past and to think of the issues of race relations as having arisen simply as a consequence of post-war immigration (Hall, 1978). But, inevitably, historical perspectives condition present attitudes and reviewing the curriculum needs explicitly to be concerned with ethnocentric assumptions which, however indirectly or obtusely, may, by reflecting past discriminatory attitudes, sustain present prejudice. Decisions about the curriculum are taken within a largely taken-for-granted framework of assumptions which draw on Britain's history and present social structures. In so far as there is racism embedded in those assumptions, it is possible for those making seemingly straightforward choices about what to include or exclude to slip into unintentional racism (Jones and Kimberley, 1982).

Assessing materials

Assessing teaching materials for racism and stereotyping is an example of the need for conscious reappraisal of accepted practices. This is an area in which there has been considerable activity in recent years. In Britain, as in other countries, many sets of criteria for the evaluation of bias and negative racial stereotyping have been produced (see Hicks, 1981). There are also now numerous compilations of recommended books and resources for different age groups (for example, Klein, 1982). A survey of multi-racial schools in 1980 showed that there was considerable awareness of the issues among teachers (Little and Willey, 1981). Heads of Departments commented that while wholesale replacement of biased and outdated materials was not practicable – nor necessarily desirable – much could be achieved by teachers' attitudes and approaches and by the way they handled material with their pupils. Typical comments were:

> Our ideas of bias and discrimination are changing .... I think that negative racial stereotyping is becoming more and more perceived. The teacher has to be aware of the problems and try to deal with them as they arise.

> These questions are carefully considered by us as a Department when purchasing new books ... pupils are taught to question material at all times and textbooks are used critically.

We have looked at our stock, especially older books, with racial bias and negative stereotyping in mind, but not with the intention of wholesale disposal. Bias is part and parcel of teaching history and such books, dealing for instance with the growth of the British Empire are useful examples of outdated attitudes.

But the issues are much less perceived in schools with few or no minority ethnic group pupils. As the National Union of Teachers argues:

the teacher in the all white school needs to be doubly aware of the problems of stereotyping; it is here that the misleading stereotypes of other groups which children receive from their textbooks will have no contradiction in reality and may be unthinkingly accepted ... these children need to have assimilated in school positive experience of the diversity of cultures to be found elsewhere in Britain. (NUT, 1979)

Organization and staffing

There has long been recognition of an urgent need to increase the number of black teachers and administrators at all levels of the education service. This is considered in Chapter Four, where forms of 'affirmative action' are discussed. But some of the routine ways in which schools can encourage more black participation in the education service are suggested by the relevant section of a checklist complied by Berkshire LEA (1983b) in relation to its policy statement on education for racial equality. To encourage recruitment of ethnic minority teachers and governors, schools are asked to consider:

1 Do advertisements for vacancies emphasise commitment to racial equality and justice, and are they therefore likely to attract applicants from ethnic minorities?
2 Is close knowledge and experience of an Asian or Afro-Caribbean community seen as a positive and relevant qualification for certain appointments?

3 Are ethnic minority teachers encouraged to apply for promotion and secondment, and do they in fact apply?

4 In secondary schools, is teaching specifically commended as a career to be considered by Afro-Caribbean and Asian young people, and by their parents and communities?

5 Do ... representatives on the school's governing body reflect the ethnic composition of the community which the school serves? If not, what steps has the governing body taken to co-opt ethnic minority members?

As Spears argues in relation to the United States, racism can be 'in its most powerful instances covert, resulting from acts of indifference, omission, and refusal to challenge the status quo' (Spears, 1978). An individual, or a school, may not have deliberately, or indeed consciously, acted in a prejudiced way but 'need only to have gone about business as usual without attempting to change procedures and structures in order to be an accomplice to racism, since behaviour as usual has been systematised to maintain black and other minorities in an oppressed state'. Schools have to counter the effects of such institutionalized racism – which are often less obviously apparent and more intractable than direct prejudiced behaviour – over a wide range of aspects of school organization. Newsam gives the following straightforward example of how indirect discrimination may operate (Newsam, 1984). Suppose a school has a rule that pupils who are suspended can return only if a parent comes to school with the child at a given time in the school day. On the face of it there is nothing unreasonable about such a rule. But suppose, because it does not believe problems go away if you choose not to notice them, the school also notices that a disproportionate number of black pupils are among those who are out of school longest because a parent has not complied with the rule. If it is then discovered that a high proportion of black parents cannot get permission to leave their jobs in the way the school's rule requires, where does this leave the school? As Newsam argues:

> The obligation on the school is to try to change the rule which is having a discriminatory effect. Sometimes the change will be possible; sometimes it will not. A 'racist' institution is quite simply one in which discriminatory rules or systems apply and no one has either noticed or tried to remove them.

Another example of the way in which racism may operate through forms of school organization is in relation to processes of selection and grouping. There has been considerable criticism of the education system over recent years for discriminating against certain pupils by unfair processes of selection and grouping. This can occur where there are 'nurture groups', banding or streaming, or withdrawal groups, and in the selection of examination groups in secondary schools. It is essential to ensure that no selection of these kinds is affected by conscious or unconscious stereotyping of an ethnic group or black pupils, and in multi-racial schools such procedures have consistently to be reviewed (ILEA, 1983b).

Teacher attitudes

The process of assessing the consequences of past discriminatory attitudes which may be deeply embedded in curriculum assumptions and forms of school organization brings teachers up against the need to examine their own attitudes. The National Union of Teachers in its pamphlet on *Combating Racialism in Schools* stated that 'Teachers have a powerful responsibility to combat ignorant and prejudiced attitudes amongst their pupils' and urged teachers to 'lead by example' in seeking to 're-educate their pupils in more positive social attitudes' (NUT, 1981). But a prerequisite for assuming such a role is that teachers consider and analyse their own attitudes. Experience in schools which have worked on developing anti-racist approaches suggests that it is important to start from the basis that the attitudes of the staff, as well as the institutional practices of the school, have been developed in a society where racism has a central influence. Teachers themselves reflect attitudes in society and for this reason, as the Rampton Report repeatedly stressed, they must be prepared critically to examine their own attitudes (Rampton, 1981a). As Rampton wrote in an article written after the publication of the Report:

> The racism to which we have drawn attention affects everyone everywhere. It is something of which too many of us are still too guilty. If we speak of self-examination we are thought to be moralising; if we recommend self-criticism, we sound as if we are cultural revolutionaries. But how else can we persuade ourselves to change our attitudes? (Rampton, 1981b)

Teacher expectations and stereotyping

The Rampton Committee was convinced from the evidence it received that racism, both intentional and unintentional, has a direct and important bearing on the educational performance of some West Indian children. Part of the reason for this was that some teachers had 'stereotyped or patronising attitudes towards West Indian children, which, when combined with negative views of their academic ability and potential, may prove a self-fulfilling prophecy' (Rampton, 1981a). Earlier research had also found evidence among teachers of 'large scale stereotypes of West Indian pupils' (Brittan, 1976), and it has been argued that there is a need to examine the way in which negative attitudes may operate in different ways against minority ethnic group communities, for example in the stereotyping of West Indian children as 'disruptive' and 'slow' and Asians as 'passive' (Green, 1982). Such stereotyping can operate not only through direct hostility, or more hidden versions of it, but also in more subtle ways. Marland warns that what is more worrying, because it is less obvious and more difficult to deal with, is well-meaning low expectation. 'Unhelpful stereotypes are hard to fight, and are more powerful when unacknowledged – or created in well-meaning warmth, for then the very kindness is denying the teaching style required' (Marland, 1980).

A study by Carrington and Wood of 'Hillsview' comprehensive in the North of England illustrates the effects such stereotyping can have (Carrington and Wood, 1983). The study was designed to analyse the social processes accounting for different rates of participation between white and West Indian pupils in extra-curricular school sport. Thirty-two per cent of the pupils in the school were of West Indian background and these pupils were 3.7 times more likely to participate in extra-curricula sport than white pupils. The researchers found that this over-representation in sports teams was in part the outcome of channelling by teachers who had a tendency to view this ethnic group as having 'skills of the body rather than skills of the mind' and as creating disciplinary problems. These teachers did not appear to the researchers as overtly hostile to ethnic minorities or 'intentionally racist'; indeed, they were 'liberal minded' and regarded themselves as non-racist. But the manner in which they behaved was 'racist in consequence rather than intent' (Wellman, 1977). Responses to the question 'Do you vary your approach in the classroom to suit pupils of different ethnic backgrounds?' indicated that teachers held lower expectations of West Indians and were prepared to tolerate lower standards of academic work and behaviour from them. Typical comments were:

> I attempt to give West Indians room for manoeuvre when they are not conforming. I give them as much work as possible because even the able West Indians become agitated when not writing well.

> West Indian children dislike doing helpful tasks, they consider one is treating them as slaves …. I am prepared to

accept louder or noisier behaviour from West Indian pupils than Asians or other groups.

Other teachers at 'Hillsview' operated with a more clearly apparent framework of racial stereotypes – describing West Indians as a group as 'lacking in ability', 'unable to concentrate', 'indolent', 'insolent', 'disruptive', 'aggressive' and 'disrespectful of authority'. Although these teachers often expressed negative opinions about the behaviour and academic abilities of West Indians, they often commented that this group did well in low-status, practical activities. West Indian pupils were variously described as having a 'well developed sense of artistic ability' or 'greater athletic prowess than white pupils', and as being 'ideal for dance and drama' or 'capable of achieving better results physically than educationally'. Several teachers made explicit reference to what have been characterized as 'the physiological myths surrounding black athletic success' (Gallop and Dolan, 1981). For example:

> The physique of West Indian children generally would appear to be in line with getting better results at sport. (Humanities teacher)

> West Indians are superior in the power they can generate compared to white kids. They seem to possess better musculature and don't have the fat you often find on a British kid. (Science and PE teacher)

> Sport gives them a chance of success. Whereas they're not successful in the classroom, they can show their abilities on the sports field. (Humanities teacher)

Carrington and Wood also found that some teachers in the school directly cultivated the involvement of disaffected non-conformist pupils in extra curricular sport as a means of social control.

The extremely influential and pervasive effect of teacher expectations on pupil performance in general was highlighted in a 1980 HM Inspectorate report on the ILEA. The report stated, in relation to the overall low attainment of pupils within the authority, that 'schools frequently blame their pupils' backgrounds for the poor results' but the Inspectors' view was that 'this is largely unjustifiable. The fault lies in low teacher expectation' (DES, 1980). Such low teacher expectation is undoubtedly a significant element in the low attainment of some black pupils. One local study into the 'serious underachievement' of West Indian pupils reported significantly that on the question of teacher attitudes 'there was a tendency for black members of the working party to stress teacher attitudes and for white members to consider them of minor importance. This difference may simply be a reflection of the different perceptions and realities of life for black and white people in Britain' (Black Peoples Progressive Association and Redbridge CRC, 1978).

SUMMARY

This chapter has argued that positive change should be introduced into schools to dismantle racist practices and to reassess underlying attitudes and assumptions. This needs to be built into formal school policies and made integral to teaching practices. Such policies need constantly to be sharpened and refined. As with most processes of introducing educational change, it is necessary systematically to monitor whether stated aims are being realized and objectives achieved. In 1981 the ILEA's 'Multi-ethnic Inspectorate' produced an *Aide-Mémoire* for use by the authority's Inspectorate as a whole (ILEA, 1981a). This included a series of questions relating to racism which 'should be considered by all schools'. These questions are an example of the sort of framework which can be adopted for reappraising practices and monitoring developments, and they summarize much of what has been covered in this chapter.

Have racism and its damaging effects been examined as a focus for developing and agreeing on a school policy or consensus?

What strategies are used for responding to incidents such as:

— racist name-calling
— writing of graffiti
— circulation of racist literature
— racialist attacks and conflicts
— the activities of organised racist groups?

Having recognised obvious incidents, are staff also aware of the impact of more covert forms of racism on their pupils?

— for instance, have they considered the circumstances within the school which may preclude pupils of particular ethnic groups from achieving their potential?

How is the school taking steps to combat racism?

— within the objectives, content and activities of the curriculum
— through extra-curricular activities
— through counselling?

Are staff encouraged, within their classrooms as well as outside their areas of direct responsibility, to:

— recognise antagonisms and conflicts at an early stage
— develop strategies to guard against them
— find and share ways of resolving them?

What support is given to teachers and pupils in developing strategies to combat racism by:	— the head — senior staff in the school — staff with particular knowledge and experience?
Does the school create opportunities for staff and parents to meet and discuss aspects of racism with:	— individual parents when particular incidents have occurred — larger groups to look broadly at the issues?

Chapter Three
'Whole-school' approaches

Emphasizing equality focuses attention on the extent to which dismantling racism must be the central concern of teachers. Developing positive responses to ethnic and cultural diversity is an integral part of this process. What is required is not a disparate package of optional 'multi-cultural' extras, but the development of good educational practice relevant to a society committed to equality. Because of the deeply entrenched influence of racism and of ethnocentric attitudes and assumptions teachers have to reappraise a wide range of their existing approaches. This confronts them with a difficult task. Permeating teaching with opposition to racism and with positive responses to ethnic diversity is difficult to approach, complex to work out and taxing to implement. But unless it is achieved, the classroom experience of children will remain little affected.

This chapter looks in more detail at what is involved for teachers and at how schools are responding. In schools where successful developments have taken place 'whole-school' approaches have often been adopted and teachers find that complicated educational decisions have to be made. This chapter argues that there is need for wide debate of the issues by teachers. The type of support which schools require is then examined. If real change is to be effected, response is necessary from the education system as a whole; in the final section of this chapter the need for initiatives from the examining boards is considered as an example of how action in schools must be accompanied by comparable developments elsewhere in the education system.

Early initiatives

During the 1970s individual teachers were undertaking a variety of forms of curriculum innovation in multi-racial schools – introducing wider perspectives into history and geography, teaching 'World Religions', discussing race relations in social studies. 'Black Studies' programmes were developed in a number of secondary schools. In a variety of forms these teachers examined with their pupils such issues as contemporary black–white relations in society, the causes of black immigration, the histories and cultures of the Caribbean, Africa and Asia. A considerable amount of important innovatory developmental work was undertaken. But such teaching was usually the result of the initiative of an individual or a small group of teachers – even if supported by a sympathetic head – and was carried out at the periphery of the mainstream curriculum. It was often non-examination work, or was included in areas such as General Studies which allowed considerable scope for individual project work. A common pattern was to develop syllabuses for Certificate of Secondary Education (CSE) Mode 3 examinations, which enabled teachers who were prepared to contribute considerable time and effort to develop special units relevant to particular groups of pupils. In general, response to minority ethnic groups was seen as a matter for particular and additional provision, and largely by default became the responsibility of concerned and committed individual teachers.

Official policies: 'permeating the curriculum'

When the shift from assimilationist to pluralist objectives took place in the 1970s, the change was often expressed in official policy in terms of new approaches to the curriculum. In 1977 the Canadian Minister of Education – in language which is virtually interchangeable with that used at about the same time in Britain, Australia and America – called on teachers 'to ensure that all our curriculum guidelines and support documents maintain a multi-cultural perspective. We are striving for a multi-cultural dimension in all curricula' (Ministry of Education, Ontario, 1977). Such sentiments were echoed in other quarters, for instance by the teacher unions. In Britain the NUT stated that responding positively to ethnic diversity should be a 'naturally accepted part of school life' (NUT, 1981); for the Assistant Masters and Mistresses Association 'an awareness of the multi-cultural society in which we live and the place of that society in the world community is so essential a dimension to learning that it should permeate the whole curriculum' (AMMA, 1981). At the level of policy declaration this change in direction generally continued the emphasis on culture, largely divorced from the realities of racism, which was discussed in Chapter One. But comparable changes in approach were also taking place in schools, and among teachers curriculum development has increasingly been informed by the need to deal with the issues of prejudice and discrimination.

Developments in schools

A Schools Council survey of 255 multi-racial secondary schools (Little and Willey, 1983) found that there was a wide degree of acceptance on the part of head teachers and heads of department of the view that responding to ethnic diversity was – at any rate theoretically – a responsibility of the school as a whole (Little and Willey, 1983). In 68 per cent of the schools the issues were discussed at meetings of senior staff or all staff. Where more than 30 per cent of the school's pupils were from minority ethnic groups such discussions took place in 90 per cent of schools. Ways of responding to ethnic diversity were also widely debated at department level – for example, by 90 per cent of English departments, 80 per cent of history and home economics departments, 60 per cent of geography departments, and 40 per cent of biology departments. Many replies from heads of departments indicated that such discussions were a constant, on-going feature of the work of their departments.

The level of debate in schools represents a considerable change from the position in the early 1970s when responding to the presence of minority ethnic groups was largely regarded as the specialist preserve of a few teachers. What is significant is the degree to which there is increasing acceptance that ethnic diversity has general implications for schools. It is when there is detailed examination of the issues by teachers with classroom experience in multi-racial schools that the artificial divorce between responding to culture and race, which is so often suggested in official policies, is most likely to be broken down. The nature, quality and extent of the curriculum development work being undertaken by schools which was reported to the Schools Council project varied considerably. Some replies suggested that responses were largely tokenistic, others that the teachers involved were primarily preoccupied with aspects of cultural difference. In some schools there was evidence that teachers were engaged in thorough and painstaking review both of curriculum content and of the influence of racism on underlying assumptions and practices. But the fact of increasingly widespread debate is important in itself. It is when the issues are opened up in schools that the complexities of the educational questions which arise emerge, the need for explicit strategies to combat racism is made apparent, and 'whole-school' approaches are recognized to be necessary.

Curriculum development

Replies from the Schools Council survey (Little and Willey, 1983) showed that the type of curriculum development being undertaken within many secondary school departments was less concerned with adding and replacing discrete units of relevant content – as it had been in the 1970s – and more with new approaches to the curriculum as a whole. Teachers considered that responding positively to ethnic diversity should be a natural and integral part of the curriculum they taught. The shift towards this wider perspective is apparent in the following quotations from heads of departments' written replies to the project's questionnaire. These examples have been chosen because they are broadly representative of approaches now being adopted in a considerable number of secondary schools. The teachers involved have not necessarily thought out systematic strategies for combating racism, but they have embarked on the sort of detailed consideration of established practices which can lead to recognition of the scale of change which is required. It is from the basis of the sort of work now taking place in an increasing number of classrooms that more comprehensive policy approaches have to be developed:

Head of an English department:

As Britain is a multi-cultural society all school curricula should reflect this. In English we have a specific responsibility to ensure that the world as we present it through literature and in discussion is a fair representation of our environment. The process of increasing sensitivity to other people is developed naturally out of literature and topics and the discussions which arise from them. It is a process of permeation to give all children a sense of identity with their own ethnic background through the different aspects of the English curriculum. This is a continuing concern of the Department, and the syllabus is being shaped to take account of, and to allow expression of, the ethnic diversity of our pupils.

Head of a history department:

Britain is and will remain a multi-cultural country. The curriculum should attempt positively to break down the negative stereotypes which each group has of the other. It should also attempt to allow each group's self esteem to grow and flourish by the study of their own cultural development and the development of the cultures of others. 'Multi-culturalism' is with us and the positive aspects of this fact should and must be made manifest within schools' curriculums.

Head of an art department:

The diversity of art, design, dress, food, music, which is to be found within the ethnic minority groups can greatly enrich the various areas of experience included in my faculty. Staff need to be encouraged to take an interest in the life and styles of these groups; both indigenous children and those of the ethnic minorities need to be made aware that the teacher recognises the merits of the minority culture. As the subject matter of the Art curriculum centres on the individual and his or her own experience the presence of minority ethnic groups in British society will of necessity be integral to our curriculum.

Head of a biology department:

Our curriculum aims to promote an awareness of racial differences and their origins and to explain these in terms of the biological principles of variation, evolution, natural selection and adaptation to environment. We have discussed, as a Department, how to avoid racial stereotyping and causing offence regarding religious or other observances and beliefs. We are also careful in our choice of illustrations of physiological and biochemical phenomena.

Comparable innovation is taking place with nursery, primary and junior children. In the 3–7 age range, for example, many approaches now concentrate on infusing the existing curriculum and school ethos with a multi-cultural constant. Accepting existing methodology and the underpinning principle of child-centredness, attempts are being made to examine ways in which positive responses to ethnic diversity can be introduced. In one LEA which has developed a project for primary schools designed to incorporate both the Bullock Report's recommendations on language and materials and 'the promotion of multi-cultural education throughout all schools in the Authority', response to cultural diversity has been seen as central to the 'core' curriculum debate (McFarlane, 1980). The approach has been to reassess existing themes used for basing relevant class projects across curriculum areas, such as maths and science, art, needlework, history, geography, religious education and games, as well as the more obvious storytelling, comprehension and literacy skills. One of the teachers described the rationale behind her approach:

> Multi-cultural education is not something to be tackled as a one-off project and then forgotten. It is a continuing process: the books we use, the pictures we display, the topics we study, the festivals we celebrate should all reflect the diversity of the people and cultures of Britain today. (Willey, 1982)

Confronting the issues

It is once the practicalities of a pluralist response to ethnic diversity begin to be examined in depth at school and departmental level that complex educational questions arise for teachers to which the rhetoric of official policy provides no readily applicable answers. Difficult decisions have to be made, for example, about the degree and nature of the diversity which the school should encourage and endorse and the relationship of this to the need to provide pupils with the knowledge and understanding which they require to operate in the world outside school. It is at classroom level in multi-racial schools that the divergence between pluralist ideals and the realities of contemporary society have to be confronted. Teachers are faced by the need to consider how 'multi-cultural-ism' can be made a rational educational ideology in a society whose institutions are not necessarily geared to tolerant pluralism (see James, 1979). Vague injunctions from policy makers about harmony and mutual tolerance have to be translated into rigorous, professional curricula approaches to racism. Teachers have both to educate children in positive attitudes towards diversity and teach them about how and why the society in which they live actually functions. A growing number of the teachers developing the sorts of approaches outlined above are coming to accept that teaching about discrimination and race relations has to be a natural and integral part of contemporary education. Some would no doubt accept Hall's formulation that

> Instead of thinking that confronting the question of race is some sort of moral intellectual academic duty which white people with good feelings do for blacks, one has to remember that the issue of race relations provides one of the most important ways of understanding how this society actually works and how it has arrived where it is. It is one of the most important keys, not into the margins of society, but to its dynamic centre. (Hall, 1980)

In constructing an educationally valuable curriculum which is relevant to a pluralist society, teachers also have to accept the need for appraisal and evaluation of different cultures. As Zec warns, a sentimental 'valuing' of all aspects of a culture which are different from a teacher's own can be as anti-educational as ethnocentrism: 'we could not be said to be taking our own or other cultures seriously if we were only prepared to think critically – that is evaluate after reflection – either only about another culture (ethnocentrism) or only about our own (cultural relativism)' (Zec, 1980). Educational judgements have to be made. Teachers are recognizing that, as James argues, their job is not 'the passing on of cultures as if it were in lumps – white lumps, black lumps, or multi-cultural lumps', rather it involves developing in children the ability to deal with the diversity of human ideas, achievements and experiences 'so that they are able to consider the ideas and work of any person of any social group with an unprejudiced understanding, to work out their implications, to judge their merits and demerits on justifiable grounds and to use them in the creation or re-creation of their own cultures and ways of life' (James, 1982). As James says, in practical terms for teachers this means looking for distinctive features of a child's own experience in the expectation that these will be more likely to be supportive than destructive, more likely to have a rational basis than an irrational one, and so potentially are more likely than not to be starting points for educative processes. It is not surprising that questions such as these lead teachers into complex, protracted and sometimes contentious debate.

The importance of debate in schools

When the complexities of translating broad pluralist intentions into curricular realities become apparent – as they are in an increasing number of schools – it is clear that change cannot be brought about by the vague formulations of official policy. It can only be achieved if opportunities are provided for wide discussion of the issues by teachers.

A respondent to the Schools Council survey commented:

> Teachers have to be involved in the planning of a syllabus suited to the needs of our multi-ethnic school population because they are the ones who will teach it. Present such a syllabus as a fait accompli and no matter what good intentions underlie it, its successful implementation will be difficult if not impossible. (Head of geography department)

This is true of curriculum development in general. Whatever the outcome of the debate about freedom and uniformity in the curriculum, major decisions about what is taught and how it is taught will continue to be made by teachers. Effective curriculum change depends on developmental work by practitioners. But the need for wide teacher involvement is particularly important in relation to working out responses to cultural and racial diversity. This is partly because there will be a wide divergence of attitudes within schools which need to be freely and openly expressed and (as far as is possible) reconciled in corporate policies and teaching approaches. Extensive discussion is also necessary if the complex educational issues which arise are to be opened up, analysed and resolved. As one head teacher put it:

> I believe that teachers have to develop *their* philosophy in these matters and that contact at national level, reading, research, etc. questioning their own and their colleagues' ideas is perhaps one way in which they can come to terms with the fact that society is an ongoing thing and that often it acts back on the creators of the next generation. The multi-racial society believes in our ability as educators and we must not betray that confidence.

'Whole-school' approaches

Many of the heads and heads of departments who reported to the Schools Council survey that they considered that a comprehensive approach was necessary across a range of school activities were under no illusions about the complexities of what this involved. It was seen as requiring a systematic review of existing practice in which staff should be as widely involved as possible. In one Manchester comprehensive where a working party of teachers spent two years examining 'the whole work and ethos of the school in the light of its multi-cultural nature', the conclusion was: 'There is an over-riding need to pursue positive policies of cultural awareness across the whole of school life. Multi-cultural education will not just happen, rather prejudice and institutionalised discrimination will dominate.' In this school the working party made detailed recommendations to the whole staff on wide-ranging aspects of school life. Their proposals covered teachers' attitudes and expectations, in-service training, social education, tutor group work and community education, school assemblies, extra-curricular activities, school departments and syllabuses, examinations, community contact, support services and monitoring and attainment (Birley High School, 1980).

Setting up a working party to consider priorities relevant to a school's particular situation was a common practice reported to the Schools Council survey: 58 per cent of schools with 30 per cent or more minority ethnic group pupils had established such working parties, which acted as a focus for initiating and sustaining wider discussion among staff. Another example is a comprehensive school where the heads of department meeting set up a working party which produced a series of questions which they considered 'every teacher in the school should ask him/herself ... and then compare notes within a department'. The questions included such things as consideration of underlying bias and stereotyping in attitudes and teaching approaches, examination of the appropriateness of textbooks and materials and analysis of the performance of minority ethnic group pupils as individuals and as a group. Each department in the school was then asked systematically to consider the implications for their department and to 'see how well or ill-equipped they are for this, and what developments would be helpful' (Wood Green School, 1979).

This sort of procedure can create a framework in which 'whole-school' approaches can be developed which provide teachers with the opportunity jointly of contributing to working out an overall school policy. In an increasing number of schools such initiatives are resulting in explicit recognition of the need to combat racism and to develop pluralist objectives and incorporate them into the formal aims of the school. Inevitably the process is often highly contentious. In the Manchester comprehensive referred to earlier, Birley High School, the staff working party acknowledged that as they undertook their work:

> It rapidly became clear that we had not adequately explained our aims to the staff as a whole. Partly because of prejudice and emotion ... the working party faced formidable antagonism and suspicion. The atmosphere of cynicism towards the work was substantial and became overt at several meetings.

A report from a junior school describes how:

> Discussions were long and argumentative. This reflects the difficult task the group faced, as aspects of multi-culturalism tend to be controversial issues. The attitudes of individuals, their assumptions about themselves, their school and the community varied considerably. (ILEA, 1981a)

The head of a London comprehensive where staff were just beginning to take the view that 'our multi-cultural work should be much more firmly embedded in the daily classroom experience of students' summed up what she recognized was needed:

> The real and positive developments in a school, involving staff at all levels with democratic debate and decision making, is a slow, difficult and sometimes painful process.

As well as curriculum review our systems of organisation need examination. Having stated our aims and begun the business of analysing our practice, we need to invent, criticise and modify as we go along. (Wilson, 1983)

A complex and difficult process is involved. But it is only through this sort of steadily widening and deepening self-examination by staff of themselves and their school's practices that the dismantling of racism and the establishment of positive responses to diversity can begin to be achieved.

Support for schools

It is teachers who have to play the central part in clarifying objectives and developing appropriate practice – individually, within subject departments, on a 'whole-school' basis and in conjunction with colleagues in other schools. To be able to do this effectively they need concerted support from the education system. Only a small number of schools have as yet undertaken systematic review of their teaching. For many teachers constraints of time and resources – and in some cases uncertainty as to what action to take – severely limit the progress they are able to make. Typical comments from teachers to the Schools Council project were:

The whole area is difficult; I recognise the need to develop a new approach and feel the need for proper expert advice.

We don't pretend to know a lot of the answers. We are puzzling our way through and find it very frustrating that there is so little professional expertise around.

I feel that as with other people in the field we are still seeing through a glass darkly. It is but an embryonic albeit vitally important field.

We need resources and specialist support. The issues have been identified … but there is a limited amount we can do without much further help.

One head of a history department gave expression to a feeling present in very many of the replies from teachers; the help which was most needed was time: 'Time for a school to sit down and work out a philosophy; time to sit down and examine the issues; time for teachers' assumptions and expectations to be laid bare and challenged'.

Local education authority response

At LEA level the provision of adequate and appropriate support for schools means developing altogether new approaches to the presence of minority ethnic group pupils. This is because one of the consequences of early preoccupation with meeting E2L needs was that the pattern of organizational provision built up within authorities was geared to developing specialist language teams. And although it is now recognized that pluralist aims have far-reaching implications for many aspects of school life, local authorities have often responded by simply extending the nominal responsibilities of their language teachers. Specialist E2L services are asked to take on wider responsibilities for curriculum and resource development and are transformed into 'multi-cultural support services'. But although in a small number of authorities increased resources have been committed which enable the new service realistically to tackle its wider role, often the additional responsibilities are in practice simply tacked on to the functions of overburdened E2L specialists seconded to schools. Language services are given a general remit to develop 'multi-cultural education' and language specialists are asked to take on additional functions such as encouraging response to cultural diversity among their staffroom colleagues, providing advice on resources and initiating curriculum development. These are things which already hard-pressed E2L teachers do not necessarily have the time, expertise or experience to carry out.

By the late 1970s a growing number of LEAs were recognizing that a different and more substantial response was required. A fairly typical example is Haringey. In 1978 the authority decided that encouragement of appropriate curriculum development in schools required specialist support which could not be provided through the language service. A separate 'Multi-cultural Curriculum Support Group' was set up. This new team circulated a statement of aims and objectives to all teachers in the authority and initiated a programme of visits to schools to discuss with teachers the proposition that 'The multi-cultural curriculum is one which is appropriate to the education of all pupils' (Borough of Haringey Education Service, 1981). The Support Group now undertake a wide range of development projects which have originated from requests made by schools, heads, subject departments and individual teachers. Another example of changing LEA response is the ILEA. The process of developing the new policy approaches discussed in Chapter Two began in 1977 when a general review of 'the issues involved in providing an education in today's multi-ethnic society' was conducted. As a result, substantially strengthened administrative and inspectorate provision was introduced 'in order to provide the necessary support and direction for all who are working with the many aspects of our multi-ethnic education policy' (ILEA, 1977). A main aim of the new approach was to provide more effective support for initiatives being taken by teachers. Two years later a progress report reiterated the priority of initiating and supporting wide debate of the issues within schools and in the local communities. The context in which increased specialist curriculum development resources were to be provided was the belief that 'the issues of a multi-cultural society must be seen by London teachers as central to providing good education for all children' (ILEA, 1979).

Permeating general educational provision

The development of specialist support services for schools is essential. But implementation of pluralist aims requires much more than the creation of special teams to assist teachers. As Woodruffe, the ILEA's Senior Inspector for multi-ethnic education, has emphasized 'the development of policy into practice has to be a priority in *all* branches and parts of an LEA' (Woodruffe, 1982). This view is shared by many of the special 'Advisers for Multi-cultural Education' appointed by LEAs. The role of such Advisers has changed. Many now emphasize that in addition to being responsible for seeing that their authority meets the particular needs of minority ethnic group pupils, they are increasingly turning their attention to influencing their colleagues in the advisory service and through them mainstream educational provision. They see a major part of their function as being to encourage their colleagues to discuss the implications of cultural diversity during their normal work with teachers. As one Adviser who has argued that 'the major priority is to have a review of the curriculum and to avoid an adding-on mentality' acknowledges, this approach has implications for the authority as well as for schools – there is a need for 'acceptance of ... an integrative approach by all officers of the authority'. (Little and Willey, 1983)

In 1981 the ILEA's specialist 'Multi-ethnic Inspectorate' published the *Aide-Mémoire* on *Education in a Multi-ethnic Society* referred to in Chapter Two. The way in which this document was handled within the authority provides an example of the vital transition which has to be made in the perception of educational responses in a pluralist society. In introducing the publication to the Inspectorate as a whole, Birchenough, at the time the authority's Chief Inspector, noted:

So far the approach in responding to the challenge of education for a multi-ethnic society has been to develop and use additional criteria, rather than to redefine those which we have been applying to the educational system.

This aide-memoire ... has been drawn up on the premise that since we serve a multi-ethnic population, our existing criteria must be re-examined and developed in such a way as to recognise that fact. (ILEA, 1981a)

A central dichotomy in permeating the education system with responsiveness to ethnic diversity is the need to avoid the setting up of specialist provision leading others to consider that this absolves them from taking action themselves because they can leave it to the 'experts'. As a head teacher has put it:

The central problem is that if attention is concentrated on the needs and interests of particular ethnic minorities, as is often the case, and understandably so, many teachers do not see the relevance of multi-cultural education to their teaching as a whole. (Little and Willey, 1983)

The examination boards

An example both of the importance of making responses to ethnic diversity integral to educational approaches generally, and of the limited extent to which this has as yet been achieved, is provided by the examination boards. Many secondary teachers who have been attempting to respond to exhortations to make their curriculum relevant to pluralist objectives reported both to the Rampton Committee and to the Schools Council project that they are constrained in what they can do by the requirements of the examination system. Teachers consider that minority ethnic group pupils are disadvantaged both by the types of language required and by the content of the syllabuses. Typical comments were:

Second language children have very great difficulty in understanding and using technical and idiomatic terms without which most examinations are closed to them.

Almost all GCE and CSE Mode 1 exams are culturally biased in favour of indigenous pupils.

Examinations restrict relevant curriculum development very considerably ... the traditional stances are adhered to in examination courses.

The whole curriculum needs re-examination but is heavily dependent in secondary schools on public examination syllabuses.

The examination boards for their part largely take the view that it is up to teachers to take the initiative. The boards argue that 'examinations follow the curriculum' and that they cannot attempt to bring about changes until all teachers are prepared for them. But, in practice, curriculum development at secondary level is closely related to examination requirements. Examination syllabuses may not be intended to be teaching syllabuses but they exert a powerful influence which extends to age ranges well below the fourth and fifth secondary years. Although the boards claim that they are flexible and responsive to teachers' needs, syllabuses have altered very little to take account of the ethnic diversity now present in society. The Rampton Committee had 'some remarkably parochial responses' from the boards; one commented:

The board is aware that some schools and colleges have special problems because of their multi-ethnic school populations. These problems would appear to relate to teaching difficulties arising from different background experience or cultures and to social integration. They do not appear to relate to examinations.

Another board commented: 'While it would be foolish to claim that all syllabuses were culture free ... the Board would maintain that where they are not, the inherent culture is and should be British.'

Although a more positive approach is being taken by some CSE boards, the emphasis remains firmly on action by teachers rather than on any direct initiatives by the boards themselves. Many of the CSE boards said that they considered that Mode 3 provided adequate and appropriate opportunities for teachers to develop units for use with particular groups of pupils – an approach directly at variance with the view that pluralist concepts should permeate the curriculum as a whole.

Teachers individually cannot reorientate the curriculum; they need sustained support. But Gill has shown that to a considerable extent geography syllabuses – to take one example – often perpetuate rather than challenge distorted and discriminatory attitudes. A group of third form pupils in an ILEA secondary school, when asked about their images of the 'Third World' listed the following: poverty, babies dying, monsoons, war, devastated crops, starvation, disease, drought, refugees, flies, death, Oxfam, dirty water, India, Cambodia, curries, beggars, malnutrition, bald children, large families, insects, stealing, poor clothing, bad teeth, kids with pot bellies, mud huts, injections (Gill, 1983a). All too often the distorted overall picture built up from such images – which are powerfully projected in the world outside school – are implicitly endorsed by examination syllabuses and by the textbooks written to support them. In a detailed study of twenty 'O' level and CSE geography syllabuses Gill found that fourteen presented the developing world 'almost exclusively in terms of problems', while most of the urban geography syllabuses were at best 'irrelevant to the needs of a multi-cultural society' (Gill, 1983b).

The examination boards must themselves take the initiative. And this means much more than the inclusion of token questions in particular examination papers; it involves systematic and sustained reassessment, subject by subject, of the assumptions underlying existing syllabuses. One examination board which replied to the Schools Council survey – the only one which reported having undertaken a significant initiative –

gave an indication of how the process can be started. The board had asked all its Subject Advisory Panels to prepare detailed reports on the ways in which they considered that an ethnically diverse society had relevance to their work, and on the action they proposed to take. Without this type of response from the established institutions of the education system real progress towards implementing pluralist aims in classrooms will remain limited.

SUMMARY

The development of pluralist aims for education has led to a shift from preoccupation with meeting the particular needs of minority ethnic group pupils to recognition that response should permeate educational provision as a whole. At classroom level in multi-racial schools progress is being made and experience is revealing that building positive responses to ethnic and cultural diversity into teaching is a complex process. Teachers have to play a central part in translating broad pluralist objectives into classroom practice. If they are to do this effectively they require support – through specialist help in areas such as curriculum development, through in-service training, and, in particular, through being given opportunities for detailed discussion with colleagues. And if the principle of permeation is right for schools it has also to apply throughout the rest of the education service. Only if the issues are seriously addressed in a context which sees them as integral to providing good education for all children will theoretical objectives really begin to shape children's educational experience.

Chapter Four

Particular needs and positive action

Combating racism and developing positive responses to diversity should be an integral part of teaching in all schools. The earlier chapters of this book have been primarily concerned with ways of developing good educational practice relevant to all children in a multi-ethnic society. But in addition provision is needed to meet the particular needs of minority ethnic group pupils – for example, those who speak English as their second language. Positive action is also required to counteract the effects of racism which result in black people being disadvantaged as a group. This chapter considers policy responses to these needs and the case for 'positive discrimination' in education.

Although there has been recognition of the need for specific strategies to counter what the Commission for Racial Equality in Britain has characterized as 'the disadvantages experienced by racial minorities which spring from racial prejudice, intolerance and unequal treatment in society', this has made little impact on the approaches pursued by the DES (Little, 1978). In this chapter evidence of the way in which black pupils are achieving in schools is considered and the response of the education system is examined. The principle that the most socially deprived should have proportionately the most support is firmly enshrined in many aspects of educational practice, but despite this there has been sustained reluctance to apply this to minority ethnic group pupils. Finally, attention is turned to the United States where very different approaches to 'positive discrimination' have been implemented. It is argued that the American experience has important lessons for Britain and elsewhere.

The need for positive policies

In both Britain and America the fact that racial discrimination results not only in prejudiced acts against individuals but in black people being disadvantaged as a group has been recognized by public policy. In Britain this was argued in the 1975 Government White Paper, quoted in the Introduction, which spoke of a need for positive policies to prevent 'an entire group of people' being 'launched on a vicious downward spiral of deprivation' (HMSO, 1975). This view reflected what a number of research reports had been saying over the previous decade – that the particular consequences of racial discrimination would not necessarily be ameliorated by general policies to cater for disadvantaged groups in society but would require specific, precisely targeted responses (see Little, 1978). In America the Civil Rights Acts of the 1960s were followed in the 1970s by the introduction of policies of 'positive discrimination' and 'affirmative action' programmes. Although the analysis of the need for specific action to counteract the effects of racism has been similar in both countries the strategies adopted have varied considerably, as will be seen later in this chapter.

In Britain a report to the Home Secretary from the (then) Community Relations Commission in 1976, attempted specifically to answer the question of 'the extent to which the needs of ethnic minority communities differ from those of the rest of the population in areas of urban deprivation' (CRC, 1977; Cross, 1978). The report, based on a review of existing research including detailed analysis of census data and on interviews with 'policy makers, practitioners and lay persons', concluded that there was widespread recognition that there were special issues relating to the disadvantage of ethnic minorities. Lord Scarman, in the report on the official inquiry into the Brixton disorders in 1981, came to the same conclusion. There was a need for direct and positive intervention. What was required was not more of the same but particular policies designed to counter particular disadvantages:

> If the balance of racial disadvantage is to be redressed, as it must be, positive action is required. I mean by this more than the admirable approach adopted by at least some central and local government agencies at present, which is intended chiefly to persuade the ethnic minorities to take up their share of general social provisions. Important though this is, it is not, in my view, a sufficient answer. Given the special problems of ethnic minorities, exposed in evidence, justice requires that special programmes should be adopted in areas of acute deprivation. (Scarman, 1981)

The concept of 'positive discrimination' in education

The idea of 'positive action' and 'special programmes' of the kind called for by Scarman is not new to British education. Educational policy has in practice long accepted that equality of opportunity means 'more and different for some' if equal access to educational chances is to be a reality for all. In many ways the concept of discriminating positively in favour of the disadvantaged is entrenched in the education system – the idea was enshrined in the Plowden Report (HMSO, 1967), the Rate Support Grant has been weighted in favour of urban areas, Educational Priority Programmes have been developed and Social Priority Schools established. The ROSLA programmes, Schools Council and other curriculum projects, schemes for differentially allocating central and local government funds, and for building up support services around schools, have, with accompanying secondary school reorganization, all been influenced by the philosophy that more should go to those who face most difficulty. Indeed, Shipman has argued that 'the common element in much educational policy in the last twenty years has been positive discrimination' (Shipman, 1980).

In the 1960s the concept of positive action was dominated by the notion of compensatory education. This was the view that intensive educational programmes should be designed to give help to students disadvantaged, for example, through poverty or family background. A damaging and dangerous consequence of applying this approach to minority ethnic group pupils has been a tendency to stigmatize black family structures and forms of black culture as being in themselves deficient or deprived. Theories of 'cultural deprivation' or 'poverty of culture' were advanced. This thesis implicitly assumes that attention should focus on remedying deficiencies in children rather than examining the way in which educational institutions function. The result has been to obscure the way in which racism subordinates ethnic groups and so to sidestep the most important political issues.

An example of the 'pathology' explanation of black disadvantage is the much cited and controversial Moynihan Report (Moynihan, 1965). Moynihan, whose writings when Assistant Secretary for Labor in the United States in the mid-1960's had considerable and damaging effects, argued that black males were victims of past racist practices (i.e. slavery) and that therefore the black male accepted a matriarchal family structure because of the supposed legacy of emasculating slavery. This form of family structure was, of course, not consistent with the patriarchal norms of American society and was therefore a primary cause of social disadvantage. The consequence for policy was that 'a national effort towards the problems of Negro Americans must be directed towards the question of the family structure'. This analysis led to schemes such as 'Operation Headstart', a comprehensive programme for pre-school children from disadvantaged backgrounds to 'break the cycle of poverty'. This type of compensatory response, with its theoretical bias of remediation, has since been extensively criticized and largely discredited. It has been unable to document long-term changes in children's cognitive development. But the central point is that this whole approach is, in Labov's words, 'designed to repair the child, rather than the school; to the extent that it is based on this inverted logic it is bound to fail' (Labov, 1973). Instead, as has been argued in earlier chapters, attention must be turned towards the ways in which black people are disadvantaged because of present forms of racism and present forms of structural inequalities.

But criticism of compensatory approaches does not invalidate the need for positive action. Over recent years there has been increasing recognition that the effects of racism require specific policy responses. The need for intervention has been comprehensively documented and extensively argued. Given that the principle of such action is in many ways inherent in British education, how have minority ethnic group pupils fared in British schools and what has been the response to their needs?

Achievement of minority ethnic group pupils

No systematic study has been made of how West Indian and Asian children are achieving academically in British schools. But there has been a considerable amount of localized work which has been reviewed by Tomlinson (1980; 1983). Mortimore has also undertaken a review of the most important work available (ILEA, 1983b). Both these studies emphasize that the variables affecting the educational performance of different minority ethnic group pupils, and the differences between them and white groups, are complex. Conclusions from such research studies as there have been must be cautious and tentative.

Tomlinson has detailed the results of thirty-three studies of West Indian educational performance and nineteen studies of Asian educational performance which have taken place since 1966. The studies fell into two main types, those using individual psychometric tests, ostensibly to measure 'ability', and those using group tests to measure performance. A few studies examined success in public examinations and school-leaving qualifications, and official statistics and some research indicated the position of minority ethnic children in school 'streams' and in 'special' education. Overall, as Tomlinson emphasizes, the data must be treated with caution. The use of conventional psychometric tests for minority ethnic group children has been extensively criticized, usually on the grounds that the tests or test situations are culturally biased. Some studies using teacher assessment have also been criticized because they have been carried out without considering the effects of teacher expectation and perception of minority ethnic group children.

Given such important reservations as these, Tomlinson's overall conclusion was that 'As a great many commentators have noted – both small- and large-scale studies using individual and group tests indicate that the performance of "immigrant" children tends to be lower than that of indigenous children.' Although minority ethnic group children born in the UK were doing better than the immigrant children, they were still not performing as well as their white contemporaries. West Indian scores tended to be the lowest of all ethnic minority group scores. Significantly, there was in particular 'to date no evidence that "A" level performance will allow ethnic minority children to move into higher education or professional training "equally" with indigenous children'. Of the thirty-three studies of West Indian educational performance covered by Tomlinson, twenty-six showed the children to score lower than white children on individual or group tests or to be over-represented in ESN(M) schools and under-represented in higher school streams. Of the nineteen studies of Asian educational performance, twelve indicated a lower score than whites on individual or group tests, or under-representation in selective schooling or fewer 'O' level or CSE passes than whites.

In the early 1970s particular concern focused on the extent to which the effects of discrimination were responsible for a long-term disproportionate placement of West Indians in schools for the educationally sub-normal. Coard attributed the causes not only to unsuitable tests but to low teacher expectations, teacher stereotyping, cultural bias and the low self-esteem and self-concept of black children in a hostile society (Coard, 1972). No official figures on the number of West Indian children in ESN(M) schools have been available since 1972. At that time the statistics showed 0.5 per cent of Indian and Pakistani children in such schools, compared with 0.6 per cent of indigenous children and 2.9 per cent of West Indian children. But although the DES claimed in 1977 that the trend was being reversed (HMSO, 1977), research has shown that while the proportion of children in the general school population in such schools is 0.5 per cent, the proportion of West Indian children is 2.5 per cent (Tomlinson, 1982). This study also found that whereas it took an indigenous child two years on average to reach ESN(M) school, passing through the assessment procedures, it only took an 'immigrant' child 11.4 months on average.

Concern is also mounting about possible over-representation of West Indian children in the variety of disruptive units, withdrawal classes and guidance units which have developed on an *ad hoc* basis during the 1970s. A survey in the ILEA showed that pupils of African/West Indian origin formed 28 per cent of the population of such units but only some 15 per cent of the comparable age group in the general population; a further 7.5 per cent of children in the units were of mixed parentage (ILEA, 1981b).

Attainment in public examinations

In 1981 information on school-leaving qualifications was made available by the Rampton Committee Report. This included the results of a DES survey of school leavers' qualifications in six urban LEAs which covered some 50 per cent of the school leavers of minority ethnic group origin in the country. The survey indicated that in 1978/9 Asian and white pupils did between twice and six times as well as West Indian pupils at 'O' level, and six times better at 'A' level. Only 1 per cent of West Indians went on to university compared with 3 per cent of Asians and 3 per cent of other school leavers, and 1 per cent of West Indians went on to other full-time degree courses compared with 5 per cent of Asians and 4 per cent of other leavers (Rampton, 1981a). These figures have been criticized as being understandardized; for example, they provide no breakdown for such important factors as parental social class or educational level (Reeves and Chevannes, 1981). As the Rampton Committee acknowledged:

> At this stage in our work we are not in a position to evaluate this information or to take into account the complex network of similarities and differences that would allow us to draw comparisons between the achievements of Asian and West Indian pupils.

But the broad conclusion to be drawn from the figures – and the one relevant to educational policy makers concerned with the effects of discrimination and disadvantage – is that drawn attention to by the committee – 'our concern is that West Indian children *as a group* are underachieving in our education system'.

As Mortimore comments in his overview:

> there are no simple explanations for differences in the
> academic achievement of pupils from ethnic minorities.
> Although there are some pointers – for example, in the area
> of language and in the negative effects of racism – more
> detailed research is needed to provide clearer answers.
> (ILEA, 1983a)

He makes the important point that such research should
investigate causes of success, not just failure. For example, in
the ILEA a study of pupils of West Indian origin, banded in the
top transfer group to secondary school in 1977, is being
undertaken which may shed light on these issues. But, overall,
it is clear that at present West Indians as a group are
underachieving. What has been the education system's
response?

Official responses: general policies for the 'disadvantaged'

Despite the effects of racism, the DES has consistently taken
the view that any particular needs which ethnic groups may
have will, by and large, be met adequately through general
policies designed to alleviate deprivation and disadvantage.
The overall rationale was spelt out in a Government reply to a
Parliamentary Select Committee in 1974:

> Where immigrants and their descendants live in the older
> urban and industrial areas, the majority of their children are
> likely to share with the indigenous children of these areas the
> educational disadvantages associated with an impoverished
> environment …. The pattern of special help must thus
> provide for all those suffering educational disadvantage.
> (HMSO, 1974)

But the point being pressed by the Select Committee – and it
was to be made increasingly forcefully in a series of subsequent
reports and research studies – was that black children, in

addition to the extent to which some of them might share aspects of disadvantage with other groups in society, had particular needs which arose from the effects of discrimination and which required particular remedies.

In 1977 the Parliamentary Select Committee, after a further inquiry, again stressed what was by then all too obvious: 'the relative underachievement of West Indian children seriously affects their future employment prospects and is a matter of major importance both in educational terms and in the context of race relations' (HMSO, 1977). A 'central educational fund' was needed to assess and meet this group's particular needs. The DES again turned this down. The Department's thinking remained that 'as the most fundamental needs of ethnic minorities are essentially the same as those of the population as a whole, it is through the general expenditure programme of central and local government that these needs should be met' (HMSO, 1978).

But by this stage the DES was prepared to acknowledge that 'as well ... as sharing in the general problems of urban deprivation and unemployment, the West Indian community and other ethnic minorities have certain special problems which we call by the shorthand term "racial disadvantage" '. Although the effects of racism were well known, and there was important emerging experience in schools of how to combat its effects, the result of the DES's partial conversion to a possible need for positive action was the classic bureaucratic response – a Committee of Inquiry was set up. In 1981 this committee produced an Interim Report (the Rampton Report) which urged the need for a comprehensive 'programme of action' directed specifically to the needs of West Indians (Rampton, 1981a). Running throughout the committee's recommendations – on pre-school provision, on reading and language, on the curriculum, on teaching materials, on links between school and community, on teacher education – was emphasis that policy and provision must focus more closely on particular needs. The committee explicitly criticized the linking of minority ethnic groups' needs with those of other disadvantaged groups in society:

> Within the DES itself we have been concerned to note that the needs of ethnic minority children are often seen only as an aspect of educational disadvantage or in some cases just a form of handicap. This seems to reflect a general view throughout the education service that ethnic minority children are a 'problem' and in some way 'lacking' or 'inadequate'.

But no action has been taken on the Rampton Report's recommendations. The need for positive action has not been recognized in official educational thinking. As has been shown in Chapters 2 and 3, there has been action in some multi-racial schools but it has not provoked official response nationally. These local initiatives need wide-ranging support, for example, through the systematic examination of the effects of racism throughout the education service, through the setting up of resource centres and the development of learning materials to assist work in schools, through the provision of appropriate in-service courses. Overall, what is required is a comprehensive interventionist approach to dismantling racism.

Additional resources

There has been some measure of additional resource provision to multi-racial LEAs in Britain. This has been provided through the Local Government Act, 1966, and the Urban Programme. But consideration of the way in which these resources have been administered by central government reveals that even the limited funding made available to local authorities has not been used to develop any concerted strategy of positive action. Section 11 of the Act enables central government to pay to local authorities a 50 per cent grant (raised to 75 per cent in 1975) for 'special provision in the exercise of any of their functions in consequence of the presence within their areas of substantial numbers of immigrants from the Commonwealth whose language or customs differ from those of the community'. Grants were restricted to the employment of staff. 'Immigrant' was defined as being people resident in the UK for fewer than ten years, and 'substantial numbers' as being, in respect of educational claims, LEAs with 2 per cent or more Commonwealth immigrant pupils on their school rolls. Provision is not limited to education but in practice Section 11 has been predominantly used for claiming teachers' salaries – an estimated 85 per cent of £50 million was allocated for this purpose in 1980/1.

But although Section 11 grants are theoretically earmarked directly and exclusively for combating racial disadvantage, in practice the operation of the scheme has not enabled a targeted and effective response to particular needs. Little control or direction has been exercised over how the money is used. The Act is administered by the Home Office and the terms and procedures of Section 11 have not enabled the DES to adopt the positive leadership necessary in order to help LEAs develop new and specific forms of provision to attack the effects of racial discrimination and disadvantage at source. LEAs are not required to ensure that Section 11 appointments relate to any general appraisal of the need for special provision in their areas, or that their use is part of any concerted strategy. Authorities are under no obligation to distinguish staff paid for in this way from other staff and these appointments are often subsumed within overall staffing levels. There is no scrutiny beyond a purely financial audit, and the DES does not monitor how the grant is used. The initiative for making a claim rests with the local authority and take up has been very uneven.

There has been widespread criticism of the scheme not only by educationalists but by a Parliamentary Committee which reviewed its operation in 1981 and found: 'there is no single aspect of Section 11 payments which have escaped criticism' (HMSO, 1981b). The majority of Section 11 teaching posts are non-specialist. The Parliamentary Home Affairs Committee estimated that one in three were E2L teachers; the rest, whose occupants may or may not have had any specialist training, are simply additions to the general staffing complement in multi-racial schools. Some LEAs have used Section 11 to instigate important initiatives, and some authorities welcome the freedom of action which lack of central control and monitoring has given them. But it remains a fact that many teachers funded under the major scheme designated expressly for attacking the effects of discrimination simply merge into the general staffing of schools and are not even identifiable as meeting any specific need. As the Home Affairs Committee pointed out 'lowering the teacher–pupil ratio must be beneficial for all pupils, but Section 11 should not have become a mechanism for this simple end'.

Statistics and monitoring

Central government's reluctance to take positive action to redress the effects of racial disadvantage is exemplified by the failure to collect statistics which could act as a basis for planning effective intervention. Between 1966 and 1972 the DES collected statistics on the 'immigrant' school population – defined as pupils born outside the UK or born in the UK to parents who had been in the country less than ten years. These figures yielded little information of educational value and in 1973 collection was discontinued. But, as the Parliamentary Select Committee pointed out, 'the argument that the statistics were not satisfactory is not an argument that there should be no statistics' (HMSO, 1977). In 1978 the DES agreed to the collection of statistics 'in principle' but no further action was taken. No question on ethnic background was included in the 1981 census.

However, the 1979 Schools Council survey showed that a majority of LEAs in multi-racial areas believe that a detailed information base is essential for assessing needs in multi-racial schools (Little and Willey, 1983). In practice, many LEAs have continued to collect local statistics after the DES discontinued the requirement to do so. The main reasons given by LEAs in favour of collection were that this information would be helpful in assessing special educational needs, in allocating resources to meet them and in monitoring the performance of children of minority group origin and the functioning of the education system in meeting their requirements. Typical LEA comments were:

> We feel that only by maintaining statistics of our school population can there be an adequate basis for planning and resourcing the service as a whole and particularly schools with special needs.

> We feel that this is the only sure way to help us assess the needs and provide for them.

> This is essential; we need such information to influence the development of a multi-cultural policy. (Little and Willey, 1983)

There was emphasis that the information obtained must relate to educational needs, and that great care and sensitivity must be exercised in the method of collection, but broad agreement that this information is necessary for formulating and monitoring policy. In 1983, Morrell, the leader of the ILEA, summed up the views of many LEAs:

> Traditionally the black communities have opposed ethnic record keeping because it has been used by governments to oppress and humiliate. We hope that ... we can devise a means whereby an authority, acting in good faith, can keep such records, in order to identify discrimination and check on the allocation of resources. (ILEA, 1983b)

That the DES has preferred to operate without such an information base is indicative of official half-heartedness about pursuing an interventionist strategy.

'Positive discrimination'

The 1976 British Race Relations Act actually enshrined the principle of positive discrimination in legislation. The Act allowed for the recognition of 'special needs' and special treatment to meet them in education, training and welfare, and for 'discriminatory training'. In this context 'discrimination' meant ethnically exclusive positive discrimination. The Act specifically recognized that special measures were needed to enable minority ethnic groups to achieve equality. An obvious area in which such provisions could be applied would be to increase the number of black teachers. Many LEAs state that they attach importance to the recruitment and promotion of more black staff. But to say that, as an employer, you are in favour of equality of opportunity does not, in itself, create equality. Implementation of such a principle requires a plan of action that would include, for instance, an examination of existing recruitment and promotion procedures, the collection of data and the exploration of forms of positive action such as 'access' courses to encourage black people to enter teaching.

The 1977 Select Committee Report recommended that national action be taken to overcome the under-representation of West Indians in the teaching profession. The committee had no official figures to work on but estimated from evidence presented to them that there were perhaps 800 black teachers overall – about 0.15 per cent of the total number of teachers. The committee urged the DES 'forthwith to consider ways and means of increasing the numbers of teachers of West Indian origin in maintained schools' (HMSO, 1977). The Department responded, but on a very limited scale. A pilot scheme was set up to establish special access courses to prepare mature students, particularly but – as might be expected from the Department's overall approach – not exclusively from minority ethnic groups, to enter training for teaching and the other caring professions. An official project evaluating this scheme has shown that these courses 'present an encouraging and increasingly convincing picture of the success of this approach' (Millins, 1982). But despite this evidence, there has been no action to extend such courses. One of the most significant manifestations of racism is the absence of ethnic minorities from positions of power and decision making within the education service itself. Official action to redress this imbalance has been little more than tokenistic.

The US experience: 'affirmative action'

The cautious and hesitant approach towards the effects of racial discrimination adopted by educational policy makers in Britain contrasts strongly with action taken in the United States, where, during the late 1960s and throughout the 1970s, a concerted programme was built up – described as 'affirmative action' – which was designed to overcome the effects of past prejudice. Although the situation of minority ethnic groups in the two countries is very different, significant parallels can be drawn. In both countries initial action concentrated on legislating against individual acts of discrimination, but in both countries experience increasingly showed that the effects of discrimination resulted in black people being disadvantaged as a group in relation to whites, and that a wider social policy response was necessary to overcome the effects of past prejudice. Whereas in Britain official policy has been slow to act on this analysis, in America direct action has been taken. As some recent studies suggest, US experience may have important lessons for Britain (Robbins, 1982; Cheetham, 1982).

Affirmative action in the United States developed most fully in relation to employment. Policies were designed to reverse the 'under-utilization' of blacks – described by the Department of Labour as 'having fewer minorities ... in a particular job group than would reasonably be expected by their availability'. Affirmative action plans generally have as essential items agreement to analyse the composition of the workforce to discover direct or indirect discrimination, the establishment of numerical employment goals and timetables to redress any imbalance in the position of black workers, active recruitment of minority ethnic group employees and the establishment of training opportunities for existing minority ethnic group workers to increase promotion prospects.

Comparable approaches have been adopted in relation to education, notably – and controversially – in the form of the widespread development of special admissions programmes to institutions of higher education. Robbins cites a study of one such programme at the University of California which had been undertaken by two British HM Inspectors. Through 'outreach' work in schools and special admissions procedures the university had increased the percentage of minority ethnic group students from 13 per cent to 27 per cent over the seven years up to 1978/9; the HMIs' view was that this kind of approach 'might with value be adopted by institutions of higher education in the U.K.' (Robbins, 1982). Such programmes have aroused controversy and have been challenged in a series of cases brought to the Supreme Court by whites who have claimed that they were being discriminated against. The Court, in a complicated series of judgments, has declared against specific quotas but has in effect validated affirmative action including numerical goals and timetables and race-conscious provisions in admissions programmes. The Carter administration specifically advised universities and colleges to establish 'numerical goals to achieve the racial and ethnic composition of the student body' considered desirable. As Cheetham comments, although American experience shows that the advancement of ethnic minorities through positive discrimination provokes fierce debate and continuous reassessment of its legitimate parameters, it is not claimed there that the costs are greater than the price of continuing gross inequalities. (Cheetham, 1982)

SUMMARY

Mounting evidence has demonstrated that a negative ban on

minority ethnic groups. Experience is also showing that the special nature and degree of the effects of racism will persist despite policies aimed at the disadvantaged generally. In Britain, although the principle of positive discrimination is widely accepted in education, it has not been effectively applied to the position of minority ethnic groups. The need for positive intervention has been accepted by successive governments at a theoretical level but this has not been followed by a concerted policy response from the DES. A consequence of weakly directed central resource allocation has been that the vast bulk of the funds committed for multi-cultural education has gone towards meeting the basic language needs of E2L learners, and that other needs have been neglected. In particular, there has been a persistent failure to assess and meet the needs of West Indians. Above all, what has been lacking in Britain is resolute national action to tackle the widespread effects of racism. There may be some lessons here in US experience. The need for the kind of affirmative action programme found in the States can be defended just as strongly and logically for Great Britain and elsewhere. Black people are being disadvantaged as a group because of the effects of racism. The present provisions are cumbersome, expensive and of unproved effectiveness. As Little and Robbins argue, simply countering discrimination will allow these patterns to crystallize; doing nothing more 'may be to accept increasing segregation continuing disadvantage, and an unacceptable degree of polarization.' (Little and Robbins, 1982)

Chapter Five

Responses to linguistic diversity

Much of the debate about education in a multi-ethnic society now centres on how combating racism and developing positive responses to diversity can be made an integral part of mainstream teaching. The shift from assimilationist approaches to pluralist aims which emphasize equality is resulting in radical changes of perception about appropriate response to bilingual and bidialectal pupils. In an assimilationist framework provision concentrated on teaching non-English speaking children English so that they could take their place in normal classes. This was often accomplished in specialist language centres separated from schools and for mainstream teachers it was largely business as usual. But in a pluralist context preoccupation with fitting minority ethnic groups into the existing system is giving way to looking at ways in which the system can respond to pupils.

Teachers are increasingly considering how they can react positively to the linguistic skills children bring with them to school. Schools are developing approaches which enable the richer linguistic diversity present in multi-ethnic classrooms to be made a positive feature in teaching the class as a whole. These moves in turn relate closely to wider discussion over recent years about the role of language in education – about ways of teaching English, about the role of all teachers as teachers of language, about the development of language across the curriculum.

These new approaches to language constitute practical ways of combating racism and developing equality in education. This is exemplified by the experience of two teachers, Burgess (a specialist language teacher) and Gore (a mainstream English teacher) who have worked on ways of collaborating in teaching English as a second language in a boys' secondary school in Brent, London. They have concentrated on developing ways of working together which act as an example to their pupils. They plan lessons together and as far as possible the second language learners attempt the same tasks as the rest of the mixed ability class. Working groups are organized which reflect mixed ability, mixed experiences, mixed first and second language users of English, and – crucially – different ethnic groups. Gore and Burgess have found:

> If not by magic, nevertheless an increasingly notable feature of the class was the growth of good relations and racial harmony. The fact is that the very strategies of openness, interaction and support which we were developing for second language learners were equally applicable to the rest of the mixed ability class. It was an unlooked for, but critical benefit of what happened when we looked for ways of teaching second language learners (that worked better than withdrawal from the mainstream): we have improved our teaching and learning processes to a point where we believe our tactics can play a part not only in school learning, but also in countering racism in education. (Levine, 1983)

This chapter looks at ways in which such newly developing approaches to language illustrate many of the themes discussed earlier in this book. Teaching English as a second language is moving back into the mainstream and this has significant implications for the education of all children. Responses to West Indian language are changing; partly because of 'unintentional' institutionalized racism the whole question of West Indian language has been almost completely ignored within the education system. Finally, attention is turned to the way in which the application of principles of equality is leading to wholly new approaches to mother-tongue and to the presence of bilingual children in schools.

The context: new approaches to language

The traditional response to linguistic diversity since the introduction of compulsory education has taken the form of attempts to eradicate it. But this has been progressively challenged. The role of Standard English and Received Pronunciation are being reviewed; attitudes towards regional dialects, often with their own distinctive sentence structures and vocabularies as well as pronunciations, are changing. There is growing interest in schools in linguistics and socio-linguistics. 'Whole-school' policies for developing language across the curriculum are being developed, requiring and eliciting greater linguistic awareness among teachers generally. The 1975 Bullock Report (DES, 1975), which played an important part in charting these new directions, specifically placed the needs of minority ethnic group pupils in the context of these wider developments. Much of the innovative work on language now taking place in multi-racial schools, where pupils' extended linguistic and dialectal range presents the issues in particularly clear form, involves new approaches to language work with all pupils. As Rosen and Burgess argue: 'The facts of linguistic diversity should oblige us to do something we might well have started before' (Rosen and Burgess, 1980).

English as a second language

The background

In Britain, providing for the language needs of children for whom English is a second language has determined both the organizational and conceptual response to minority ethnic group pupils. During the 1960s, working in the context of broadly assimilationist policy assumptions, a form of provision was established designed to enable E2L learners to enter mainstream classes with minimal disruption to existing teaching. One of the consequences of the shift to objectives of pluralism and equality has been the need to alter these organizational arrangements so as to meet altogether different conceptions about how schools should respond to children from different linguistic, cultural and ethnic backgrounds.

Rosen and Burgess have summarized early educational attitudes:

> Those children who could not speak English or who were still beyond doubt in the early stages of learning it were somebody else's business. The English as a second language teachers would give them sufficient mastery of English to equip them to enter the English as a mother tongue classroom. Once there they would be essentially no different from other pupils in the classroom. (Rosen and Burgess, 1980)

Early provision to achieve this objective varied considerably. This reflected differing local priorities and lack of experience and uncertainty about what action to take. But primarily it was a consequence of the failure of central government to take effective action to assist local authorities to develop new forms of provision.

From 1963 the DES issued a series of pamphlets and circulars offering general advice. *English for Immigrants* (DES, 1963), for example, emphasized the need for 'a carefully planned, intensive course making full use of modern methods of language teaching' and argued that at both junior and secondary level 'special classes should be staffed by teachers with some knowledge of modern methods of teaching English as a second language'; *The Education of Immigrants* (DES, 1971) referred to language teaching as 'the most urgent single challenge facing the schools'. But such exhortations largely ignored the fact that few specialist E2L teachers existed, that there were no established in-service courses to train them and limited relevant materials for them to use, and that there were widely divergent views about the degree to which specialist provision was necessary and what form it should take.

In these circumstances progress in meeting E2L needs was in practice haphazard and *ad hoc*. In 1970 when Townsend conducted a national survey of LEAs' response to immigrant pupils, he reported wide diversity both in the scale and form of the arrangements made by local authorities (Townsend, 1971). A few authorities identified those needing special help by passing every Asian immigrant child through a 'reception centre'; the more typical pattern was to rely on teachers' classroom assessments of language difficulties as they became apparent. Arrangements for instruction varied markedly. There was a wide range of full-time and part-time language classes in special centres or within pupils' own schools, organized along different lines and pursuing a wide variety of teaching approaches. Some authorities made quite substantial provision, others gave virtually no special support. Townsend commented optimistically that there was a 'welcome variety of practices'; in the experience of most classroom teachers provision was woefully inadequate.

Developing LEA provision

During the 1970s, providing for basic E2L requirements continued to be the main priority in local authorities' response to a multi-ethnic society. Experience and expertise were gradually built up, and two broad developments occurred. Provision became better organized – usually in the form of a centrally co-ordinated specialist team of E2L teachers – and the attitude that second language teaching could be largely divorced from work in normal classes was steadily modified. When a Schools Council survey reviewed provision in 1980, it was apparent that authorities were confident that significant advances had been made. In general, language teachers were working in a closer relationship to classroom teachers. E2L teachers were usually members of an identifiable specialist service but, particularly at secondary level, spent their time seconded full-time to schools. The existence of a corporate language team enabled the language teachers to retain a specialist identity within the school, rather than in practice being swallowed up as supernumerary members of staff, and to meet together on a regular basis for in-service work and to develop resources and monitor progress (Little and Willey, 1981).

But although by the beginning of the 1980s most local education authorities with concentrations of E2L learners had built up effective provision to assess and meet basic E2L needs, progress had been slow. If provision of central resources had been better targeted and monitored, and evolving good practice better disseminated, local effort could have been much more effectively directed. In one authority which had, in 1978, just reorganized its E2L provision by appointing a Head of Service to centralize the teaching force, a senior officer acknowledged to the Schools Council Project that for the first time they were now in a position not only to provide an effective service, but would be able to find out just what needs were in a way that had hitherto not been possible. This was some twenty years after substantial numbers of non-English speaking children had begun to enter the authority's schools (Little and Willey, 1983).

Meeting advanced E2L needs

A common motivating factor behind many of the detailed local arrangements reported to the Schools Council project in 1979 was the desire to secure the greatest possible flexibility between work in the language group and attendance in normal classes, and for close co-operation between the language specialist and subject teachers. This marked a significant change in attitude from the approach prevailing in the 1960s. The head of one E2L service, writing in 1981, has described this change:

> Over the past fifteen years the views of teachers working in multi-lingual classrooms have changed – from seeing children who speak English as their second language as a problem requiring some kind of specialist 'therapy', to recognising that children are learning from all around them and particularly from other English speaking children. This is not to say that specialists are unimportant – far from it – but to signal a welcome gradual change from the state of affairs where children are withdrawn from the class or even the whole school for some 'mysterious work' which the class teacher is expected to follow up ... there is a growing movement towards the specialist being in support of the class teacher. (Parr, 1981)

But although there has been a distinct shift towards making E2L provision more closely related to mainstream classroom practice, there have been limitations on the extent to which teachers have been made aware of their pupils' second language needs. This lack of progress shows up in particular in relation to meeting the more advanced needs of E2L learners – often referred to as 'second phase' E2L. The language needs of E2L learners do not end when they have a basic understanding of English. Initial provision may do little more than enable pupils to survive in normal classes, without giving them the real level of linguistic skills which they need to operate on equal terms within them. In 1971 Townsend identified the need for continuing specific support during the advanced stages of second language learning as a matter requiring urgent attention. But at the end of the decade the Schools Council project's survey found that meeting 'second phase' language needs continued to be regarded by both administrators and teachers as a major priority for action. The survey found wide agreement amongst those responsible for teaching E2L that current provision for the more advanced stages of language work and for teaching specialist subject language – which were seen as being of crucial importance to academic achievement – were inadequate. There was reported to be urgent need for the development of effective methods of diagnosing needs and monitoring performance; 80 per cent of head teachers who replied to the survey from schools with a concentration of pupils of Asian origin (10 per cent or more) drew attention to the need of many of these children for continuing language support during secondary education.

New approaches in schools

A number of authorities and schools stressed in replying to the Schools Council survey that the most effective response to advanced E2L needs was explicitly to recognize them as part of the language across the curriculum strategies emphasized in the Bullock Report. Continuing E2L needs are inevitably carried into normal classes, and if schools are to respond adequately, staff generally need to consider the implications of second language learning for their teaching. In some schools teaching approaches have been developed involving close and flexible co-operation between language specialist and class-room teacher. The work jointly being developed by the two teachers, Burgess and Gore, quoted at the beginning of this chapter, is an example of this. They emphasize that

> What has become salient for us is that this mode of working together, of collaborative learning, is a mode and an attitude of mind that needs to permeate not only pupil–pupil interactions but also those between teachers and pupils, and teachers and teachers.
>
> … working in groups with the teachers acting as consultants as well as leading the class or working in support groups became our principal mode of working. Second language learners then had access both to pupil–teacher talk and pupil–pupil talk. (Levine, 1983)

The very considerable benefits which developing these sorts of approaches can have not only for E2L learners but for children in a class as a whole are illustrated by the comments of another teacher who has been working in a similar way with a language specialist. Describing the more advanced language needs of second language learners he says:

> It's very hard for me as a mainstream teacher to identify their [English as a second language learners'] problems with English and know how I can help them. The ESL teacher was able to convince me of the enormous task that an ESL learner has to take on when s/he is learning English. This awareness has also made me more conscious of what the native English speakers are also dealing with in schools. I now feel I'm able to help them when things go wrong – especially those kids who don't speak or write bourgeois English. (*Issues in Race and Education*, 1983)

This teacher also feels that this type of approach to language work can play an explicit part in a school's response to racism. The work he has undertaken with the language teacher was also important as part of the anti-racist offensive in the school. There's been much staff discussion about this but little has happened in the classrooms. You see in mainstream lessons the white kids need to see that the teacher is concerned with the learning of the ESL kids – most of our ESL kids are Bangladeshi – so it is a sort of positive discrimination in front of the white kids. From the teacher's side it is also necessary to break down the division between what in my school they call 'the Paki teacher' and the 'real' teachers.

School policies and support

It is this type of developing awareness in multi-racial schools which relates closely to the strategies put forward in the Bullock Report (DES, 1975). Bullock's central recommendation was that all teachers should be aware of

(i) the linguistic processes by which their pupils acquire information and understanding, and the implications for the teacher's own use of language;

(ii) the reading demands of their own subjects, and ways in which the pupils can be helped to meet them.

To bring about this understanding every school was urged to develop a policy for language across the curriculum. The responsibility for this policy 'should be embodied in the organisational structure of the school'. All teachers need to be aware of their role as teachers of language, and at secondary stage all subject teachers should be conscious of the linguistic demands which their specialisms make on pupils. In multi-racial schools it is increasingly being recognized that responsiveness to the needs of second language learners is merely an extension of this developing conception of educational good practice. The approach to meeting E2L needs has shifted from being considered as a specialist concern essentially divorced from mainstream classes, to being recognized as an inevitable part of the work of all teachers in multi-lingual schools. But, as has been argued earlier in relation to so many aspects of bringing about positive change in response to a multi-ethnic society, the development of such language strategies depends on positive action from central and local government – resources for schools, additional language teachers, in-service support, 'positive discrimination' in assessing and meeting urgent needs. As the teacher quoted earlier puts it: 'In reality in my English department there is a very simple truth – if ESL provision is really to be taken seriously we must have the money to resource it – without that it's all hot air, it's just tokenism' (*Issues in Race and Education*, 1983).

West Indian language

The Bullock Report urged a major reappraisal of teachers' attitudes towards, and assumptions about, language and its use. The Report was explicit that

> The aim is not to alienate the child from the form of language with which he has grown up and which serves him efficiently in the speech community of his neighbourhood ... we emphasise that the teacher should start where the child is and should accept the language he brings to school ... and this takes us firmly to the need for an explicit knowledge by the teacher of how language operates. (DES, 1975)

This has important implications not only for speakers of British dialects of English but for the complex forms of linguistic variety present among West Indian pupils. As with the advanced needs of E2L learners, current practice is increasingly seeing response to West Indian language as an integral part of approaches to language diversity generally. But this follows a long period of sustained neglect. Throughout the 1960s and 1970s the fundamental question of whether immigrant West Indians had particular language needs in relation to using Standard English forms was almost completely ignored.

The background

It was broadly assumed by policy makers and resource providers that West Indians required no particular attention because they were basically English speakers. Any initial difficulties would be a temporary phenomenon, Standard English would be picked up in the playground. The complex questions of the differing relationship to Standard English forms of the wide range of creole, patois and dialect forms used by the immigrants were largely disregarded (Edwards, 1979). When Townsend reviewed the position in 1971 he found that West Indians with specific language difficulties in relation to Standard English were often being placed in lower streams alongside retarded indigenous pupils with quite different needs. Virtually no attention had been paid to analysing West Indians' needs or to devising forms of provision to meet them. Townsend's conclusion was that if urgent action was not taken 'there is likely to be an increasingly high proportion of West Indian under-achievers both in school and in employment' (Townsend, 1971). But by this time forms of provision were being developed which were firmly preoccupied with the specific issue of teaching E2L – and the West Indian language question was clearly outside the remit and expertise of the E2L specialists. The DES failed to give priority to directing parallel attention to West Indians, and local authorities continued to use the extra resources available to them under Section 11 of the 1966 Local Government Act to meet the more obviously apparent needs of E2L learners. In 1980 a Schools Council survey found that there was little evidence that more than a handful of authorities had made serious efforts to evaluate and meet the language needs of their West Indian pupils. This has consistently been a low priority and the report on the survey's findings argued that there continued to be 'an urgent need to clarify the extent to which and the ways in which pupils of West Indian origin have particular language needs, and to provide guidance and support to teachers' (Little and Willey, 1983).

Uncertainty about how to respond in schools

Over the period during which the West Indian language question has been neglected, the particular needs of West Indian pupils have changed. The vast majority of West Indian children now in schools were born in Britain, and the issue has become less a need to teach the Standard English necessary for academic success than to adopt positive responses to continuing and changing dialectal diversity. But the consequences of the absence of positive action at either central government or local education authority level is that there is now widespread uncertainty among teachers about what action to take. Seventy per cent of head teachers who replied to the 1980 Schools Council survey from schools with a concentration of West Indian pupils (10 per cent or more) said that these children did have particular language needs and often commented that resources and expertise to meet them were not available and that this resulted in these pupils underachieving. But there were considerable differences of opinion about the extent to which the problem was one of differences between dialect and standard forms; a number of teachers took the view that the use of patois or dialect forms was symptomatic of an assertion of identity rather than of any inability to use Standard English, and that the appropriate response was to adopt a positive attitude to linguistic diversity rather than for specialist language provision.

The Rampton Committee found similar evidence of confusion among teachers, and characterized attitudes as falling into three broad patterns (Rampton, 1981a). The first was a 'deficit' view which saw West Indian language as inadequate for learning, deficient or restricted – 'this resulted in an effort, from an early age, to change or replace the child's language, with consequent harm to his language development and self-image'. The second view was that 'dialect interference' caused difficulties for some West Indian children in using Standard English and that this required specific attention. The third group of teachers adopted a 'repertoire' approach which values all languages and dialects as an important part of the child's linguistic repertoire; the teachers' response is not to change or replace any particular dialect but to develop a sharper awareness of and interest in the different language forms that the child can use, thus avoiding confusion between them.

Changing issues

The widespread uncertainty about West Indian language is a result of the failure at both DES and local authority level to provide support and guidance for teachers. The effects of neglect cannot be quantified. The Rampton Committee's overall view was that 'we do not believe that for the majority of West Indian children in our schools, who were born and brought up in this country, linguistic factors play a part in underachievement' (Rampton, 1981a). But it is striking that the school leavers survey quoted in the report shows that in GCE English language and CSE English examinations only 9 per cent of West Indian pupils gained higher grades compared with 34 per cent of all leavers at 16+. Evidence from the 1980 ILEA literacy survey indicates that the reading attainment of West Indians was very low compared with other groups, and that not only was it low at eight years but it remained low at school-leaving age – and this is against a general background where no ILEA groups were reading at the levels expected for their age when compared with a national sample.

The Rampton Committee's fear about attaching too much importance to the language difficulties of West Indians was that these had 'too often been put forward in the past to seek to account for or explain their underachievement with the result that the more fundamental underlying causes have been neglected and avoided', and that 'whatever the degree of ... "dialect interference" we feel there is a danger that all the child's educational difficulties and lack of achievement in language might be put down to this cause'. But this should not be an argument for continued inaction – for failing to assess needs accurately and make appropriate provision. Some research has suggested that there is still 'ample evidence of creole interference' in the work of some West Indian pupils and that the problems which this causes are compounded by teachers' lack of understanding of the children's difficulties: 'unfortunately, especially in the early years of schooling, more general problems of literacy tend to mask the special problems of dialect interference ... unless the teacher is sensitive to the differences between creole and British English' (Edwards, 1979). Even if such difficulties only now apply to a minority of West Indian children resources should be allocated to enable teachers and researchers to clarify the degree and nature of such dialect interference and the extent to which the needs of West Indians differ from those of speakers of British dialects of English and require particular provision.

Positive responses

But the major need is now for schools to accord to the particular skills of West Indian pupils the kind of positive recognition – and real understanding by teachers – which the Bullock Report called for in relation to linguistic diversity generally. Work by Edwards suggests that teachers face genuine difficulties in knowing how to mark creole writing and, as a result, may confuse their pupils (Edwards, 1983). The experience of a teacher who had just begun to reassess her approach after being on an in-service course is probably broadly indicative of the uncertainty (and, on the part of her colleagues, the racism) which has resulted from the neglect of the issues by the education system:

> I'm now starting to ask myself questions that I didn't know even existed before. For example, the situation regarding West Indian patois, black English, whatever is the in-phrase at the moment. I, like many other teachers, didn't recognise

it as a language until I'd actually studied the linguistic structures of the language. Even though I am a teacher of English I'm not a linguistic expert ... but at least I know enough to be able to recognise in black English structures of a language. I have discussions on this with people in my department and even the more liberal ones amongst them don't always accept my particular point of view on this and I know other teachers I come into contact with refuse even to accept the validity of the argument; whether they agree with it or not, they still talk about jungle language, mumbo jumbo and all the rest of it. (Dunn, 1983)

Teachers' responses to language are of crucial importance. To adopt negative attitudes to language variety not only neglects pupils' abilities but can have a seriously detrimental effect on attitudes and motivation. Le Page argues in relation to West Indian 'dialect interference' that the problem is probably not now of such great importance as a direct problem as in the indirect problem which it causes (Le Page, 1981). This is that teachers, like everybody else, undoubtedly tend unconsciously to stereotype children on the basis of their language or dialect or accent. This affects all non-standard dialect speaking pupils. It has been shown that Yorkshire teachers tend to rate the academic chances of children who speak Southern Educated English (Received Pronunciation) higher than those with educated Yorkshire accents. Quebec teachers, whether English-speaking or French-speaking, rate the chances of English-speaking children higher than those of French-speakers. But the reception teachers give to West Indian language may be particularly important to children growing up in a discriminatory society — Le Page argues that 'teachers' reactions to non-standard dialects should be counteracted in the same way as their reactions to colour and class'. Sutcliffe suggests that for black British pupils creole has become a symbol which may be of great significance to young people in their teens who are establishing their own identity (Sutcliffe, 1982). Rosen and

Burgess also emphasize the importance of teacher attitudes towards West Indian language:

> what is at stake here is much more than merely tolerating the dialect of the pupil. For many pupils speaking the dialect means saying something uniquely. It may mean more. The very act of speaking it is a declaration of how and what they are and wish to be. (Rosen and Burgess, 1980)

The pioneering work of Labov and others in the United States on Black American Vernacular has shown that teacher understanding and recognition of pupils' language skills can have major benefits both in terms of supporting and encouraging confidence in learning Standard English and in positive responses to school in general (Labov, 1973). In the British context it is being argued that such approaches have relevance to schools' responses to all non-standard dialect speaking pupils (Trudgill, 1975). And – as with the advanced needs of E2L learners – West Indians' needs are increasingly being considered and analysed through the development of post-Bullock 'whole-school' language policies which are reappraising approaches to language generally. As Edwards argues,

> while there are clearly differences between the particular situations of speakers of English as a second language, speakers of West Indian Creoles and speakers of British dialects of English it is nonetheless possible to take a broad approach to linguistic diversity which identifies shared needs as well as recognising individual differences. Responsibility for the consequences of diversity can no longer be abdicated to the specialist but is a central concern of the class teacher. (Edwards, 1982)

Mother tongue

The background

Many of the general implications for schools of responding positively to linguistic diversity appear in particularly sharp focus in relation to children who speak a mother tongue other than English. Initial reaction was that the education system's responsibility began and ended with teaching these children English; their mother tongues, like the regional dialects of their indigenous peers, received little recognition. Maintaining mother tongue was seen as entirely a matter for the communities to organize for themselves – it would not impinge on normal schooling. Indeed the prevailing view was that any support for the home language would be at the expense of the child's acquisition of Standard English and consequently would be likely to hamper progress through the education system. (Houlton and Willey, 1983)

In Britain neglect of minority ethnic groups' mother tongues occurred despite experience of the provision of bilingual education in Wales. From 1970 to 1979 the number of children receiving their education in Welsh-medium primary and secondary schools more than doubled – from 8270 to 17,326 – and, in addition, many secondary schools in naturally Welsh-speaking areas offer instruction through the medium of Welsh in anything up to ten subjects. Research in Wales indicates that the minority language can be fostered without harming pupils' progress in the majority language (Sharp *et al.*, 1973). It is significant that provision in Wales has occurred chiefly as a result of sustained community pressure. But experience in Wales was not applied to the presence of other bilingual children. Throughout the 1960s and 1970s interest in minority ethnic groups' mother tongues was largely confined to helping the teacher to identify the patterns of 'interference' which were thought likely to impinge on learning English. Rarely were attempts made to support the mother tongue or to enlist it as an aid to learning; it was considered that the children's interests would best be served by discouraging the continued use of the home language in favour of a speedy shift to English. As Miller writes:

> Whereas learning a foreign language and even one or two dead ones as well has always been the sine qua non of a

'good' education, and whereas a child who picks up fluent French and Italian, say, because her father has been posted abroad, is likely to be thought fortunate, at an advantage, even 'finished', a child with two or three non-European languages, in some of which he may be literate, could be regarded as quite literally languageless when he arrives in an English school, where 'not a word of English' can often imply 'not a word'. (Miller, 1981)

New responses

Attitudes towards bilingual pupils are now changing. Increasingly classroom experience is leading to a reappraisal of earlier assumptions, particularly those concerning the child's use of mother tongue, its relationship with English and its role in learning (Houlton and Willey, 1983; Houlton, 1984). Teachers are recognizing that the particular linguistic skills and abilities of bilingual children should be seen as important educational attributes both for the children concerned and for all children in the school. Bilingualism has proved not to be a transitional phase associated with immigration; over 100 different mother tongues continue to be spoken on an everyday basis by children attending British schools. The communities have themselves sustained their languages and in many cases have developed a considerable network of voluntary language classes and community schools. There has been growing pressure from the communities for their languages to be given status and recognition.

The traditional view that support for the home language would be at the expense of a child's acquisition of Standard English is being challenged. Research evidence – in particular from the US, Canada and Scandinavia – suggests that, on the contrary, mother tongue maintenance can have positive benefits. According recognition and respect to a child's first language may be of considerable importance in reinforcing self image and self confidence, particularly during the transition from home to school. A child's mother tongue and English are ceasing to be seen as competing abilities – well developed skills in mother tongue are likely to lead to greater proficiency in English and to increase chances of educational success generally. Teachers are coming to see the child's mother tongue as providing a valuable foundation of confidence in using language and understanding how language works, and as a set of skills and resources which can be an aid to learning and to general cognitive development.

The reappraisal of responses to bilingual pupils has also been given impetus by the wider debate about diversity and equality. Pluralist objectives entail minority ethnic group parents and children being able to make genuine choices about the degree to which aspects of cultural identity are maintained, and language is central to this. Schools need to foster an environment which enables bilingual children to continue, if they wish, to make links across communities. There is growing recognition that the education system should respond positively to the wishes of parents in relation to mother tongue – that LEAs should, if requested, support community mother-tongue teaching and that schools should make provision for teaching mother tongue. In England developments in the EEC have contributed to the policy debate. In 1981 a DES circular drew LEAs' attention to their general duties under the terms of an EEC Directive to 'promote mother tongue and culture teaching in co-ordination with normal education' (DES, 1981b). Although there has been justified criticism of the EEC Directive on the grounds that in the European context the concern is more with enabling migrant workers to return to their countries of origin than with developing a pluralist approach to language and society, the Directive has in practice played a part in opening up discussion among policy makers.

The changing attitude towards mother tongue is finding its way into formulations of educational policy. The ILEA, for example, has adopted a policy towards bilingualism which lists six principles on which developments are to be based (ILEA, 1983b):

(i) It is the right of all bilingual children to know that their mother tongue skills are recognised and valued in schools.

(ii) It is educationally desirable that bilingual children in primary school should be given the chance to learn to read and write their mother tongues and to extend their oral skills in these languages.

(iii) It is educationally desirable that bilingual children in secondary schools should be given the chance to study the language of their home as a subject on the school curriculum and to gain appropriate examination qualifications.

(iv) The mother tongue skills of bilingual children should be seen as a valuable potential channel for supporting their learning.

(v) All children should have the opportunity to learn how other languages work and be encouraged to take an interest in and be informed about the languages spoken by their peers and neighbours.

(vi) In developing arrangements for teaching mother tongue and in other ways promoting bilingualism, schools should consult with mother tongue classes organised by community groups and other agencies.

Developments in schools

Working from the basic principle of wishing to build on the experiences which children bring to school, teachers are increasingly seeing the multi-lingual classroom as a rich potential resource for developing work on language with all children. Schools have begun to find out about their pupils' language skills and to investigate the wider linguistic context within which children operate outside school. Teachers can gain quite new insights into the educational experiences of their pupils. Radical reappraisals may become necessary; some teachers have found that children whom they considered to have learning difficulties were capable of operating in two or more languages. Working closely with parents and the local communities, teachers are encouraging children to use and share their knowledge of mother tongues, and are using this to lead into work with the class as a whole on different forms of language and dialect. Receptiveness to linguistic diversity is made to permeate the atmosphere of the classroom and school, and to underpin teachers' whole approach to their pupils.

In a number of schools some degree of mother-tongue teaching has been introduced, usually for young children. Such teaching may be provided in withdrawal groups, but is often integrated into the work of normal classes. The mother-tongue teacher works alongside the class teacher. This approach is leading class teachers to develop new methods of working collaboratively, not only with the bilingual mother-tongue teacher, but with older bilingual students, with parents and with other members of the community. There is also growing co-operation and consultation between mainstream teachers and mother-tongue teachers in community schools. One teacher, who works in a school which has over a number of years been developing initiatives of this sort, describes the results:

> I now find something that was difficult to find when I first worked in the school – children healthily able to 'be' who they feel themselves to be. To talk in their first language if they choose to; to talk about how they speak at home and with whom; where they were born and what they like to eat; not as a novelty, but rather as part of everyday classroom life. (Houlton, 1984)

In schools such as this responding to bilingual children is an integral part of developing good educational practice.

SUMMARY

Attitudes and approaches towards minority ethnic group language have changed considerably. Language needs have ceased to be seen exclusively in terms of teaching English as a second language and as being largely divorced from work in normal classes; a pluralist response has implications for all teachers and requires collaborative work between specialist and class teachers. The particular linguistic skills and abilities of both bilingual and bidialectal children are coming to be considered as important educational attributes both for the children concerned and for all children in the school. New approaches are being developed in the context of whole-school policies which are adopting positive attitudes towards the language variation of all pupils.

Conclusion

The way forward

In multi-ethnic societies the position of black people has consistently been regarded as marginal. Black people have been outsiders who have been discriminated against, or strangers who should be assimilated, or people whose different cultural and linguistic backgrounds should be tolerated and accommodated. The position of black people is rarely considered from a perspective which sees them simply as citizens with equal rights.

Similar attitudes have pervaded education. Minority ethnic group pupils have been seen as newcomers who must be fitted into schools with minimal disruption to existing educational practice. When more positive approaches were developed these generally remained peripheral to mainstream teaching. A common attitude has been that it would be helpful for 'culturally deprived' and disadvantaged children to receive some teaching about their customs and backgrounds; this would strengthen their poor self-image. It would also be interesting and educationally beneficial for children from the majority population to learn about exotic cultures.

But the black British – and their counterparts in Australia, Canada, America and elsewhere – are not outsiders. They are citizens. In societies committed to equality they require and demand equal treatment. Achieving this requires much more than legislating to prevent discriminatory acts against black individuals. It involves, as American experience goes some way to suggest, comprehensive examination of the way in which discriminatory attitudes and practices operate within the institutions of society. It requires positive action to dismantle the massive and cumulative effects of racism.

The same applies to schools. The most important element in responding to minority ethnic group pupils is not that they be helped to fit into the system or that their cultures are 'reflected' in the curriculum. It is that these children require, and their parents demand, good education. For schools this involves not merely assessing and meeting particular needs – important though this is – it also means rigorously and systematically examining practices and assumptions to eliminate the deeply embedded effects of racism. More positively, it means reorientating educational institutions so that they provide equality for all their pupils. From this basis the ethnic diversity of society can be made integral to the educational experiences of all children.

To bring about these changes action is required to facilitate, encourage and develop initiatives in schools. But there are wider implications. The education system as a whole must examine its practices and procedures to combat racism. Policies of positive action must be adopted across the whole of the education process. Providing equality, combating racism and teaching about diversity affect the whole work of a school, a local education authority, a national education system. At all levels procedures have to be systematically analysed, objectives defined, policies formulated and experience monitored. But it is teachers in individual classrooms who are central. It is they who implement change and it is in schools that positive educational practices are being developed.

Teachers are presented with a complex and difficult task. Schools are embedded in society and they cannot control influences on their pupils. But schools remain institutions that retain sufficient flexibility to encourage vigorous and open debate. This book has described the way in which discussion about race and equality is taking place in an increasing number of schools. The debate has been crucially — and must be consistently — informed by a black perspective. The questions which arise are complicated and the process involved in their resolution is bound at times to be contentious. But what is emerging is new ways of achieving equality and new ways of responding positively to ethnic diversity in society. These have relevance for all schools. What this book has been about is developing good educational practice for all children.

Bibliography

Allen, S. (1979) 'Pre-school children: ethnic minorities in England', *New Community*, VII(2), Summer.

Assistant Masters and Mistresses Association (1981) *An AMMA Statement: Education for a Multi-cultural Society*, London, AMMA.

Australian Department of Education (1975) *Report of the Inquiry into Schools of High Migrant Density*, Canberra, Australian Department of Education.

Australian Schools Commission (1975) *Report for the Triennium 1976–1978*, Canberra, AGPS.

Berkshire LEA (1983a) 'Education for racial equality: policy paper 1', Education Department, Reading.

—— (1983b) 'Education for racial equality: policy paper 2', Education Department, Reading.

Bhatnagar, J. K. and Hamalian, A. (1981) 'Minority group children in Canada', in Megarry, J. (ed.) *World Yearbook of Education: Education of Minorities*, London, Kogan Page.

Bindman, G. and Grosz, S. (1979) 'Indirect discrimination' in *A Review of the Race Relations Act, 1976: Proceedings of a One-Day Seminar Organized by the Runnymede Trust, London 30 March 1979*, London, Runnymede Trust.

Birley High School (1980) *Multi-cultural Education in the 1980s: The Report of a Working Party of Teachers at Birley High School, Manchester*, Manchester, City of Manchester Education Committee.

Black Peoples Progressive Association and Redbridge CRC (1978) *Cause for Concern: West Indian Pupils in Redbridge*, London.

Bolton, E. (1979) 'Education in a multi-racial society', *Trends in Education*, 4.

Borough of Haringey Education Service (1981) *Multi-cultural Curriculum Support Group. First Report, 1979–1981*, London.

Brittan, E. (1976) 'Multi-racial education 2: Teacher opinion on aspects of school life, Part 2: Pupils and teachers', *Educational Research*, 18 (3).

Carby, H. (1980) 'Multi-culture', *Screen Education*, 34, Spring.

Carrington, B. and Wood, E. (1983) 'Body talk', *Multiracial Education*, II(2), Spring.

Casso, H. J. (1976) *Bilingual/Bicultural Education and Teacher Training*, Washington, DC, National Educational Association.

Cheetham, J. (1982) 'Positive discrimination in social work: negotiating the opposition', *New Community*, X(1), Summer.

Cigler, M. (1975) 'History and multicultural education,' *Australian Historical Association Bulletin*, 4.

Coard, B. (1972) *How the West Indian Child is Made ESN in the British School System*, London, New Beacon Books.

Community Relations Commission (1977) *Urban Deprivation, Racial Inequality and Social Policy: a Report*, London, HMSO.

Cross, C. (1978) *Ethnic Minorities in the Inner City: The Ethnic Dimension in Urban Deprivation in England*, London, Commission for Racial Equality.

Curriculum Development Centre (1980) *Core Curriculum for Australian Schools*, Canberra, CDC.

Davis, A. K. (1975) 'The politics of multiculturalism and Third World communities in Canada: A dialectical view'. Paper presented to the Conference on Multiculturalism and Third World Immigrants, Edmonton, September 1975.

Davis, B. (1981) Letter to the Home Secretary, 31 July 1981, quoted in 'Nationality, children under threat', *Issues in Race and Education*, 1981.

Deosaran, R. A. (1977) 'Educational aspirations: Individual freedom or social injustice', *Interchange*, 8.

Department of Education and Science (1963) *English for Immigrants*, Pamphlet No. 43, London, HMSO.

—— (1965) *The Education of Immigrants*, Circular 7/65, London, HMSO.

—— (1971) *The Education of Immigrants*, Education Survey 13, London, HMSO.

—— (1975) *A Language for Life*, Report of the Committee of Inquiry appointed by the Secretary of State for Education and Science under the Chairmanship of Sir Allan Bullock (The Bullock Report), London, HMSO.

—— (1977) *Education in Schools: A Consultative Document*, Cmnd 6869, London, HMSO.

—— (1980) *Report by HM Inspectors on Educational Provision by the Inner London Education Authority, Summer 1980*, London, HMSO.

—— (1981a) *The School Curriculum*, London, HMSO.

—— (1981b) *Directive of the Council of Europe on the Education of Children of Migrant Workers*, Circular 5/81, London, HMSO.

Dhondy, F. (1978) 'The black explosion in schools', *Race Today*, May.

Dorn, A. (1983) 'LEA policies on multi-racial education', *Multi-ethnic Education Review*, 2(2), Summer.

Dunn, D. K. (1983) ' "Multicultural literature" in the classroom – some reactions by white teachers', *Multicultural Teaching*, 1(3), Summer.

Edwards, V. K. (1979) *The West Indian Language Issue in British Schools: Challenges and Responses*, London, Routledge & Kegan Paul.

—— (1982) *Language Variation in the Multicultural Classroom*, Centre for Teaching of Reading, University of Reading.

—— (1983) *Language in Multicultural Classrooms*, London, Batsford.

Eggleston, J., Dunn, D. and Purewall, A. (1981) *In-service Education in a Multi-racial Society: A Report of a Research Project*, Keele, University of Keele.

Gallop, G. and Dolan, J. (1981) 'Perspectives on the participation in sporting recreation amongst minority group youngsters', *Physical Education Review*, 4(1).

Ghosh, R. (1978) 'Ethnic minorities in the school curriculum', *Multiculturalism*, 2.

Gill, D. (1983a) 'Anti-racist education: Of what relevance in the geography curriculum?', *Contemporary Issues in Geography and Education*, 1(1), Autumn.

—— (1983b) 'Education for a multicultural society: The constraints of existing 'O' level and CSE geography syllabuses', *Contemporary Issues in Geography and Education*, 1(1), Autumn.

Green, A. (1982) 'In defence of anti-racist teaching', *Multi-racial Education*, 10(2), Spring.

Hall, S. (1978) 'Racism and reaction', in *Five Views of Multi-racial Britain: Talks on Race Relations Broadcast by BBC TV*, London, Commission for Racial Equality.

—— (1980), 'Teaching race', *Multi-racial Education*, 9(1).

Hicks, D. (1981) *Minorities: A Teacher's Resource Book for the Multi-ethnic Curriculum*, London, Heinemann.

HMSO (1949) *Report* (Royal Commission on Population), Cmnd 7695, London, HMSO.

—— (1967) *Children and their Primary Schools* (The Plowden Report) (Central Advisory Council for Education), London, HMSO.

—— (1973) *Education* (Parliamentary Select Committee on Race Relations and Immigration), London, HMSO.

—— (1974) *Educational Disadvantage and the Educational Needs of Immigrants*, Cmnd 5720, London, HMSO.

—— (1975) *Racial Discrimination*, (White Paper) Cmnd 6234, London, HMSO.

—— (1977) *The West Indian Community* (Parliamentary Select Committee on Race Relations and Immigration), London, HMSO.

—— (1978) *The West Indian Community. Observations on the Report of the Select Committee on Race Relations and Immigrations*, Cmnd 7186, London, HMSO.

—— (1981a) *Racial Attacks* (Report of a Home Office Study), London, HMSO.

—— (1981b) *Racial Disadvantage* (Parliamentary Home Affairs Committee), London, HMSO.

—— (1981c) *The Secondary School Curriculum and Examinations: With special reference to the 14 to 16 year old age group* (Parliamentary Education, Science and Arts Committee), London, HMSO.

Houlton, D. (1984) *All Our Languages*, London, Edward Arnold.

Houlton, D. and Willey, R. (1983) *Supporting Children's Bilingualism*, York, Longman for the Schools Council.

Inner London Education Authority (1977) *Multi-ethnic Education*, Joint Report of the Schools sub-committee and the Further and Higher Education sub-committee, London, ILEA.

—— (1979) *Multi-ethnic Education – Progress Report*, London, ILEA.

—— (1981a) *Education in a Multi-ethnic Society: An Aide-Mémoire for the Inspectorate*, London, ILEA.

—— (1981b) *Support Centres Programme – Monitoring and Evaluation Report* No. 2, 1331, London, ILEA.

—— (1982a) *Anti-Racist School Policies*, London, ILEA.

—— (1982b) *1981 Language Census*, Research and Statistics Report, RS 811/8, London, ILEA.

—— (1983a) *Race, Sex and Class. 1. Achievement in Schools*, London, ILEA.

—— (1983b) *Race, Sex and Class. 2. Multi-ethnic Education in Schools*, London, ILEA.

Issues in Race and Education (1983) 'Space to speak and work', 39, Summer.

James, A. (1979) 'The "multicultural" curriculum', *New Approaches in Multiracial Education*, 8(1).

—— (1982) 'What's wrong with multicultural education?', *New Community* X(2), Winter.

Jones, C. and Kimberley, K. (1982) 'Educational responses to racism', in Tiernay, J. (ed.) *Race Migration and Schooling*, Eastbourne, Holt, Rinehart & Winston.

Kelly, G. P. (1981) 'Contemporary American policies and practices in the education of immigrant children', in Bhatnagar, J. K. (ed.) *Educating Immigrants*, London, Croom Helm.

Killian, L. M. (1983) 'How much can be expected of multi-cultural education?', *New Community*, X (3), Spring.

Klein, G. (1982) *Resources for Multicultural Education: An Introduction*, York, Longman for the Schools Council.

Labov, W. (1973) 'The logic of nonstandard English', in Keddie, W. (ed.) *Tinker ... Tailor ... The Myth of Cultural Deprivation*, Harmondsworth, Penguin.

Lane, D. (1982) 'Chairman's valedictory', *New Community*, X(1), Summer.

Le Page, R. B. (1981) *Caribbean Connections in the Classroom*, York, Mary Glasgow Language Trust, University of York.

Levine, J. (1983) ' "Going back" to the mainstream', *Issues in Race and Education*, 39, Summer.

Lewis, W. A. (1969) 'The road to the top is through higher education – not Black Studies', *New York Times Magazine*, 11 May.

Little, A. (1978) *Educational Policies for Multi-racial Areas*, London, Goldsmiths' College, University of London.

Little, A. and Robbins, D. (1982) *Loading the Law: A Study of Transmitted Deprivation, Ethnic Minorities and Affirmative Action*, London, Commission for Racial Equality.

Little, A. and Willey, R. (1981) *Multi-ethnic Education: The Way Forward*, London, Schools Council.

—— (1983) *Studies in the Multi-ethnic Curriculum*, London, Schools Council.

Lynch, P. (1972) 'Australia's immigration policy' in Roberts, H. (ed.) *Australia's Immigration Policy*, Perth, University of Western Australia Press.

McFarlane, G. (1980) ' "Something to celebrate": Report on a primary school curriculum project in Bedford', *Education Journal* (Commission for Racial Equality), III(1), September.

McLeod, K. A. (1975) 'A short history of the immigrant student as "New Canadian" ', in Wolfgang, A. (ed.) *Education of Immigrant Students, Issues and Answers*, Toronto, OISE.

Marland, M. (ed.) (1980) *Education for the Inner City*, London, Heinemann.

Miller, J. (1981) 'How do you spell Gujerati, Sir?', in James, A. and Jeffcoate, R. (eds) *The School in the Multicultural Society*, London, Harper & Row.

Millins, P. K. C. (1982) *Progress and Performance of Students on Special Preparatory Courses*, DES Evaluation Project, London, Ealing College of Higher Education.

Ministry of Education, Ontario (1977) 'Multiculturalism in Action: A Support Document for "The Formative Years" ', Toronto, Ministry of Education.

Moynihan, D. P. (1965) *The Negro Family: The Case for National Action*, Washington DC, US Government Printing Office.

Mullard, C. (1981) *Racism, Society, Schools; History, Policy and Practice*, Occasional Paper No. 1, London, Centre for Multicultural Education, University of London Institute of Education.

National Union of Teachers (1979) *In Black and White: Guidelines for Teachers in Racial Stereotyping in Textbooks and Learning Materials*, London, NUT.

—— (1981) *Combating Racialism in Schools*, London, NUT.

Newsam, P. (1984) 'One flew over the cuckoo's nest', *Times Educational Supplement*, 27 January 1984.

Palmer, H. and Tropper, H. (1973) 'Canadian ethnic studies: Historical perspectives and contemporary implications', *Interchange*, 4.

Parr, N. (1981), quoted in Twitchin, J. and Demuth, C., *Multi-cultural Education: Views from the Classroom*, London, BBC.

Rampton, A. (1981a) *West Indian Children in Our Schools*, Interim Report of the Committee of Inquiry into the Education of Children from Ethnic Minority Groups (The Rampton Report), Cmnd 8273, London, HMSO.

—— (1981b) 'The Rampton Report: The Chairman's perspective', *Secondary Education Journal*, II(3).

Reeves, F. and Chevannes, M. (1981) 'The underachievement of Rampton', *Multi-racial Education*, 10(1), Autumn.

Robbins, D. (1982) ' "Affirmative Action" in the USA: A lost opportunity', *New Community*, IX (3), Winter/Spring.

Rose, E. J. B. *et al.* (1969) *Colour and Citizenship*, London, Oxford University Press.

Rosen, H. and Burgess, T. (1980) *Languages and Dialects of London School Children: An Investigation*, London, Ward Lock.

Rutter, M. and Madge, N. (1976) *Cycles of Disadvantage*, London, Heinemann.

Samuda, R. J. (1980) 'How are the schools of Ontario coping with a new Canadian population? A report of recent research findings', *TESL Talk*, II.

Scarman, Lord (1981) *The Brixton Disorders, 10–12 April 1981*, Cmnd 8427, London, HMSO.

Shallice, J. (1983) 'Formulating an anti-racist policy at the Skinners' Company's School', *Multi-ethnic Education Review*, 2(2), Summer.

Sharp, D., Thomas, B., Price, E., Francis, G. and Davies, I. (1973) *Attitudes to Welsh and English in the Schools of Wales*, Schools Council Research Studies, London, Macmillan/University of Wales Press.

Shipman, M. (1980) 'The limits of positive discrimination', in Marland, M. (ed.) *Education for the Inner City*, London, Heinemann.

Sivanandan, A. (1982) *Roots of Racism*, London, Institute of Race Relations.

Smith, D. J. (1977) *Racial Disadvantage in Britain*, Harmondsworth, Penguin.

Spears, A. K. (1978) 'Institutionalized racism and the education of blacks', *Anthropology of Education Quarterly*, 9(2).

Stone, M. (1981) *The Education of the Black Child in Britain: The Myth of Multiracial Education*, London, Fontana.

Stubbs, M. (1976) *Language, Schools and Classrooms*, London, Methuen.

Sutcliffe, D. (1982) *British Black English*, Oxford, Basil Blackwell.

Teaching London Kids, 'From policy to politics', No. 2 (n.d.).

Tomlinson, S. (1980) 'The educational performance of ethnic minority children', *New Community*, VIII(3), Winter.

—— (1982) *Educational Subnormality: A Study in Decision-Making*, London, Routledge & Kegan Paul.

—— (1983) 'The educational performance of children of Asian origin', *New Community*, X(3), Spring.

Toronto Board of Education (1976) *The First Report of the Working Group on Multicultural Programs*, Toronto, Toronto Board of Education.

Townsend, H. E. R. (1971) *Immigrant Pupils in England: The LEA Response*, Windsor, NFER.

Townsend, H. E. R. and Brittan, E. (1972) *Organisation in Multiracial Schools*, Windsor, NFER.

Trudgill, P. (1975) *Accent, Dialect and the School*, London, Edward Arnold.

Verma, G. K. and Bagley, C. (1979) *Race Education and Identity*, London, Macmillan.

Wellman, D. (1977) *Portraits of White Racism*, New York, Cambridge University Press.

Willey, R. (1982) *Teaching in Multi-cultural Britain*, York, Longman for the Schools Council.

Wilson, Alessandra (1983) 'The development of multi-cultural policy and practice at Walsingham School', *Multi-ethnic Education Review*, 2(1), Winter/Spring.

Wilson, Amrit (1983) 'Blame the victim', *New Internationalist*, 128, October.

Wilson, J. (1978) 'Come, let us reason together', in D'Oyley, V. (ed.) *Black Presence in Multi-Ethnic Canada*, Vancouver, Centre for the Study of Curriculum and Instruction, Faculty of Education, University of British Columbia; Toronto, OISE.

Wood Green School (1979) *Wood Green School: Report of the Multi-cultural Study Group, 1979*, London, Wood Green School.

Woodruffe, B. (1982) '1977–1982: Multi-ethnic education in ILEA', *Multi-ethnic Education Review*, 1(2), Summer.

Zec, P. (1980) 'Multicultural education: What kind of relativism is possible?', *Journal of Philosophy of Education*, 14(1).

Index